Pregnant With
JUSTICE

Pregnant With JUSTICE

Dr. D.N.N.S. Yadav LL.D.

PARTRIDGE
A Penguin Random House Company

To order additional copies of this book, contact
Partridge India
000 800 10062 62
orders.india@partridgepublishing.com

www.partridgepublishing.com/india

Contents

DEDICATED TO MY RESPECTED PARENTS, MY FAMILY
MEMBERS, MY STUDENTS AND THE LEGAL FRATERNITY
TO WHICH I BELONG. AND FOR THE CAUSE OF
JUSTICE SOCIAL, EDUCATIONAL AND ECONOMICAL
TO THE PEOPLE AT LARGE ALL ACROSS THE GLOBE
WHO ARE DENIED OF IT. SO HELP ME GOD…!!!

Preface

Pregnancy is good news but no delivery is bad news. The system being 'pregnant' with 'justice' if fails to 'deliver' even after completion of period of "gestation' than it would prove to be 'abortive'. Abortion in any form whether self-induced or a forced one is damaging for the future health of the system. 'Justice delayed is justice denied' has been an age old proverb and the justice is of no use if the victim gets it at the far end of his lifetime after a protracted trial in the courts for years and years altogether. Now the person is not in a position to enjoy the fruits of justice. One should have no feeling of any doubt about it that the people in the society are the best 'judge' despite the fact that they do not understand the very technical intricacies of law. But they do possess the finer sense of justice following the delicate perceptions of natural justice foundations. For the aforesaid reasons the justice delivery cannot escape the pinch that 'justice should not only be done but it should appear to have been done'. Where it does not appear to the people at large that the justice in fact has been done then our system passes through a phase where it has to share the burden that it would not suffice where 'only judgments are being delivered by the courts but the justice is not being delivered'.

'Delivery of judgment' and 'delivery of justice' are the two very distinct dimensions of justice delivery system in any country on this globe. It would always remain my humble submission before the caretakers of the system that 'delivery of judgment' and 'delivery of justice' should not be taken to synonymously. Justice will not be delivered unless it is 'pregnant with justice'.

'Malignant pregnancy' would ultimately amount to 'miscarriage of justice' or a 'forced abortion' of it leaving behind a 'deadly impact' on the very survival of the 'system'. We have to see that the system not only 'delivers' well but it 'survives' too. It is not only the justice delivery system or the courts but we the people also do have our bounden duty to be an integral part of the system to help it out to perform its duty. If we are doing 'wrong' knowing it well to be 'wrong' than we are to be blamed for doing injustice. We lose any moral authority unless we come with 'clean' hands.

Our justice delivery system needs a serious relook and a thorough overhauling. In the larger interest of justice world wide it is demand of the hour that 'justice delivery systems' need be stopped from being converted into a 'judgment delivery system'. Let the 'justice' be delivered...??? It needs to be ensured proper 'care' 'protection' and 'treatment' of the system 'pregnant with justice' to be able to 'deliver with justice' healthy, hale and hearty. Live long the justice...!!! On this globe.

Dr. D.N.N.S.Yadav LL.D.
Republic Day, 2015
University of Lucknow, INDIA

1

Female Feticide- It's Shameful

It is just a coincidence that I am writing this article on International Women's Day i.e. March 8. Seminars and workshops are organized to celebrate this day to uplift the dignity of the women. Every year we express our serious concern for the sake of the women but the bitter truth is that still the girl child is struggling for her survival on this earth. Existing sex ratio is an indication to this situation. Let us not deny this cruel fact that we come across newspaper reports as newly born girl babies are thrown in the dustbin by her parents, where they are eaten away by pigs, dogs, vultures etc. Killing of a girl child is shameful on part of the society. Need not to say that every girl child has a right to life. It should not be taken as any favor to her that this society is letting her live. In a patriarchal male dominated society like India female feticide is very common even today.

We never forget to stake our claim that we are an advanced, well civilized and well educated nation. But where goes our education and the so-called civilized character when we decide to kill a girl child? Have a look around the cities; you will come across mushrooming abortion clinics and pathological ultrasound centers. They display a big size board outside the clinics that "sex determination tests are crime and prohibited by law". But the truth lies in the tragedy that such clinics indulge in illegal abortions without any fear and teasing the letters of the law. Termination of pregnancy is permitted by law under strict medical supervision, with an intention to save the life of the pregnant women in the event when the doctors are satisfied that the fetus has developed some malignancy and the life of the mother would be in danger unless aborted without delay. The abortion clinics maliciously abuse the *bonafide* intention of the law and go for unlawful abortions under the bogus plea that there was a risk to the life of the mother therefore abortion was 'legally' justified.

The burning question is that as to who consents to such unlawful abortions? The obvious reply to such consents is the parents themselves. If the parents are unwilling, such clinics cannot compel them to come down to their clinics. Clinics are just professionals and we are providing them the market they need. It should be made clear that this society should not be under the expectation that the laws of the country would come up with the desired results unless the society comes forward with its hands clean and help the laws in their proper enforcement. We should not make mockery of the laws. Laws are there to control and regulate social behavior. Society should not behave in an unlawful manner just to kill its own child. Whether sons or the daughters, they should be given equal status by the society. Save the girl child. Female feticide should be condemned to its core. Human existence is not possible on this earth without the existence of the girl child. It is a social malady. Society itself would have to take initiatives to stop feticide in the greater interest of society. Let the justice be done to the female child.

"The abortion clinics maliciously abuse the bonafide intention of the law and go for unlawful abortions under the bogus plea that there was a risk to the life of the mother therefore abortion was "legally" justified."

2

Juvenile Justice- Nipped In the Bud

Administration of juvenile justice has always been a matter of serious concern in the society. The children of today are the responsible citizens of tomorrow. Every society should carefully invest in their children today so as to get rich dividends in the years to come. Any poor investment in the children will give rise to the dividends in dangerous proportions back to the society. Nationally or internationally the concept of juvenile justice goes for the care, protection, treatment, education, development reformation and rehabilitation of juveniles. It is the statutory obligation of the State to meet out the objectives of juvenile justice so that no such children are left uncared and unprotected. Do the States would admit it without hesitation that they have successfully provided the minimum standards which are essential for juvenile justice?

Let us admit the bitter truth with a heavy heart that in Indian society children are the neglected lots. Let us not deny that we have not seen children on railway stations, bus stations, cinema halls, markets, hotels and restaurants etc. begging around or selling gutakhas, tobacco pouch, doing boot polish, and doing child labor for earning their livelihood. Yes..!!!.. Their painful poverty condition is the factor which compels such children to be exposed to such unhygienic and crimogenic situations. Children are seen picking plastics, poly thenes bags and other thrown away articles from the filthy garbage disposals dumped around the city by municipality. In jhuggi-jhoparis across metro cities the children live along with their family members in worst animal like conditions. The condition of children from socio-economic weaker sections living in villages, semi-urban, sub-urban and urban areas is not much better.

Let us be honest and should not expect from such children living in such extremely adverse conditions to be the saints of tomorrow. What they are getting from the society today, they will pay it back to the society, the other day? If the society neglects them today, they will neglect the society tomorrow. Society just cannot escape from its accountability. There are negative social factors, like lack of proper socio-economic and educational development, which is a contributory factor towards juvenile delinquency. If timely proper care is not taken by the socio-political system of the country in protecting these delinquent and neglected juveniles in keeping them away from crimogenic situations then society should keep ready for dangerous consequences. The juveniles who have broken the law or who are in conflict with law, if deliberately and negligently are allowed to continue to stay in the same crimogenic environment, rest assure they will be future criminals. You just cannot stop them to be. The social system is to be blamed for all that. Social acceptability is the primary factor in care, protection, treatment, development, reformation and rehabilitation of a juvenile so that he is groomed as law abiding youth and responsible citizen. I do not wish to fall in any argument that the system has established observation, reformatory and juvenile homes for the purpose, but these homes appear to have absolutely failed to deliver the justice since they have become centers of corruption. Let us come forward and see that the juvenile justice is not nipped in the bud itself, otherwise we would not be able to save this society from future criminals.

"It is the statutory obligation of the State to meet out the objectives of juvenile justice so that no such children are left uncared and unprotected. Do the States would admit it without hesitation that they have successfully provided the minimum standards which are essential for juvenile justice?"

3

Poverty Line And Below

It has become the fashion of the day to talk about poverty line and about the people below it, by those who are at the helm of the affairs. They are busy in collecting data, drawing poverty line, arranging press conferences and addressing the problem in terms of the data so collected, with future action plan? But the bitter truth after independence is that the system has absolutely failed. The tragedy of the system is that it has performed a backward painful journey starting from poverty line to below poverty line (B.P.L.). The B.P.L. terminology is the latest creation of the system. Let us not complicate with technical definitions of poverty given by any economist. In simply layman's language where people in society are economically so weak that they are absolutely incapable to sustain their basic day to day requirements of food, clothing and shelter. There are reported instances of starvation deaths. Prime Minister of the country was deep with sorrow while talking on 'Hunger and Malnutrition' that malnutrition is national shame (2012). Poverty contributes to this pathetic situation, absolute poverty contributes absolutely.

The preamble of the Constitution of India dedicates itself to the people of India, to ensure justice- social, economical and political. It specifically mentions about its concern to counter inequality in income so as to remove economic disparity prevalent in the society. It also endeavors to the State to take measures for empowerment of the socially and economically weaker sections. In contradiction to all that the economic disparity has become much wider after independence and the rich are getting richer, whereas the poor are getting poorer with the passage of time. The question of the day is that why there are poor in the society? Where the visualizations of socio-economic justice as go enshrined under the Constitution? Should we not admit it honestly that it is all attributable to acute failure of socio-economic policy initiatives and its implementation? I am not an economist but as a citizen of this country there are genuine expectations from the existing economic justice administration system. The experts should come forward with fair economic policies to ameliorate poverty conditions from the Indian society. We have failed so far even after more than sixty seven years of independence (1947). Japan was completely ruined after Hiroshima and Nagasaki (1945) but after comparatively sixty nine years of that destruction, today they are nation with economic force to globally reckon with. It is the will power, dedication, honesty, industry, determination, sacrifice and the sense of belongingness of the people of Japan for their nation which makes all the difference, people of the world are witnessing today.

There is an affidavit before the Supreme Court of India that as per poverty line calculations Rs.32 would be sufficient for the urban poor and Rs.26 would be sufficient for rural poor for his daily needs. To my understanding this per day per capita income includes expenses on livelihood, health, education and other future exigencies as well? There could be an honest apprehension as to what extent this meager income calculation data would be in a position to justify and fulfill the fundamental needs of the rural urban poor and their very survival on this earth?

Poverty line was drawn to collect data of the people living on poverty line so that their poverty could be removed. Now we have come with 'below poverty line', which is an admission to this very fact that during these years people have gone below the earlier poverty line. It means poverty has increased and system has failed to eradicate poverty. If continuing policy implementation trends are any indications then should we be prepared to witness another poverty line to be drawn by the caretakers of the system i.e. below below poverty line (B.B.P.L.) in the years to come? No..!!! No..!!! Please let the poor now live with human dignity.

"The question of the day is that why there are poor in the society? Where go the visualizations of socio-economic justice as enshrined under the Constitution? Should we not admit it honestly that it is all attributable to acute failure of socio-economic policy initiatives and its implementation?"

———————————————

4

Penal Justice

There is a famous saying that punishment is not an end in itself, but it is a means to an end. Off course, the end is the penal justice. The concept of penal justice visualizes that even behind imposition of punishment there should be an element of justice, which the criminal justice system has to ensure. The objective behind punishments is to create fear of punishment in the mind of offenders and the people at large, so that they could be prevented from committing crimes. The greater objective is to establish a crimeless society. The objective for achieving a crimeless society has absolutely failed but still the system may feel satisfied, if there are lesser crimes in the society. The past experiences of the criminal justice system reveal that merely by means of showing fear of punishment the offenders cannot be deterred from committing crimes. Recidivists or the repeaters of the crime are one example. Most serious illustration of the recent origin is the "suicide squads" of the terrorist gangs who have absolutely no fear of punishment and they are ready to kill themselves for the sake of committing crimes.

The conclusion could be that providing punishment is not the final solution for preventing crimes in the society. For achieving the greater objectives of criminal justice, the caretakers of penal justice system should feel realize this fact that the penal administration needs infusion of 'feel of justice' behind punishments. To illustrate with, where A happens to be an honest and hard working person. Once his mother fell seriously ill. He approached the doctor. After examining his mother the doctor said to A that the condition of his mother is very serious. He should immediately give him the prescribed medicines otherwise her condition may be critical and she may die. After paying the doctor's fee, A rushed to the medical store to buy medicines for his mother. A did not have sufficient money to pay to the chemist. He requested the chemist with folded hands that please give the medicines, since the condition of his mother is very critical. He will pay the remaining amount within a day or two. If the medicines are not administered to her immediately, she may die. Despite repeated requests, the chemist bluntly refused to give medicines unless full payment is made. A was desperate, left with no other option and with an intention to save life of his mother he snatched medicines from the chemist and ran faster to his mother to administer medicines to her. Snatching away medicines is an unlawful act. A is produced before the court. He pleaded that he had no intention to break the law but under the compelling circumstances he was put in, he had to save the life of his mother. Alright..!!! Your mother was critical, but you should not have broken the law. Law will punish you for that.

Once such persons are punished and the law absolutely ignores to take cognizance of the compelling circumstances and is not considerate of it, while awarding punishment, then there is every possibility that the persons will have a loss of faith in the justice system. When he would be released from the jail after undergoing punishment, he may be converted into a hardened criminal and may prove to be cursing for the society. Since the system, while awarding punishment was never sympathetic enough to his compelling circumstances and at the same time the chemist too, being part of the society never bothered for the critical illness of his mother. Let there be a penal justice behind every punishment. Punishment is not an end in itself. Let us protect situational offenders from becoming hardened criminals. The system should take into account for the persons becoming victims of the circumstances and are compelled to commit crime without any prior criminal intention. I do not argue that they should not be punished, but they should be given judicious punishment by the system with an ultimate objective to reform such situational offenders.

"Let there be a penal justice behind every punishment. Punishment is not an end in itself. Let us protect situational offenders from becoming hardened criminals."

5

Menace of Dowry Continues

Dowry system is a social evil. Demanding dowry and offering dowry as a consideration for the marriage is deeply rooted in the Indian society. Dowry became a curse when the society started torturing and killing the married women for non fulfillment of demand of dowry. Even today, there are reported instances of dowry related physical, mental tortures and killings of the married women. Demand of dowry and offering dowry is prohibited by law. But without bothering for the law, people give dowry and demand dowry. The dowry problem is basically a social problem, it is not a legal problem and the most affected families are the middle class families. There are people who are ready to give dowry and the other party is ready to take the dowry. Now the big question is that how the law will come into motion? The person who should be aggrieved and make a complaint before law, is ready to give dowry. Despite the fact that dowry is being given and is being taken, since there is no complaint of it from the aggrieved, the law is absolutely helpless. Law needs evidence to proceed with and in the absence of any such evidence from the aggrieved the law just cannot help.

To illustrate with, I just intend to draw your kind attention to a social situation discussed herein after. I would leave it up to you to decide, as to how to deal with this social evil particularly under the circumstances where the father of a girl comes forward to help the legal system with a complaint against demand of dowry? A, who is the father of a girl goes with a marriage proposal for his daughter to B, who is the father of the groom. B demands dowry as a consideration for his son's marriage with A's daughter. A thinks B should not demand dowry since it is unlawful. A makes a complaint against B to the law enforcement agencies so that legal action could be taken against B. Now here comes the real problem. By helping the legal system of the country A has invited trouble for himself. The news that A has lodged complaint against B for demanding dowry will spread like a fire in the jungle. Wherever now, he will go with the proposal of his daughter's marriage, people in this society will disappoint him leaving him in utter frustration. He faces a threat from the society that his daughter will remain unmarried for all that he did by making complaint against the evil. Who will take this risk at the cost of one's daughter's marriage? In the absence of any such complaint from the aggrieved the law will not be in a position to help and the evil of the dowry system goes unabated. Society itself would have to come forward to eradicate this evil practice and save our girls from its menace.

Despite the fact that there is a stringent law on dowry, burning newlywed girls to death by her in laws for want of dowry is a common phenomenon in the Indian society. Subjecting her to cruelty for want of sufficient dowry is equally common. Intentionally burning women for not bringing sufficient dowry and inhumanly torturing her to death is a cold blooded murder. I fail to understand as to why the penal laws define it as 'dowry death' only, which is a lesser offence than murder? Offenders responsible for dowry killings should be put to death sentence. There are reported instances of misuse of dowry related laws as well. Innocent in-laws are falsely implicated in bogus cases abusing the process of law. The law enforcement agencies and the courts would have to be extra careful in dealing with such situations.

"Intentionally burning women for not bringing sufficient dowry and inhumanly torturing her to death is a cold blooded murder. I fail to understand as to why the penal laws define it as "dowry death" only, which is a lesser offence than murder?"

6

Gender Justice-Struggling For Self-respect

Gender based discrimination and crimes relating to women are very common in our society. Women are put to such discrimination by virtue of their birth as women. They are not treated as equal to their male counterparts. They are born equal as human beings but they are forced to be unequal by this society by virtue of their sex. Women have been put to lot of exploitation from time immemorial at the hands of male dominated society but because of nature the society is bound to admit and accept that women only are the better half of the human relationships. The issue which is serious is that as to why the women are an exploited lot in a society which claims it to be a modern, civilized and educated society? Still society behaves in a disgraceful manner and celebrates when a male child is born as compared to the female one. Despite the Constitutional position of equality of status, women are denied of their rights socially.

Administration of gender justice has different dimensions. In spite of the fact that we feel reflections of women empowerment in the society but the trail of the tragedy lies in the bitter truth that the women are even today subjected to domestic violence by this society. The Parliament had to make laws to protect the women from domestic violence. Meaning thereby, the women are struggling for self respect. Gender justice is nipped in the bud at the time when the girl child is killed in the embryo itself. Science and technological developments have not proved to be a boon for the sake of gender justice and sonographic ultrasound techniques are being used rampant for feticides. An absolute gender based injustice. The apex court of the country has taken notice of the sexual harassment of the women at the workplace. Despite definitive guidelines through Vishaka, the working women are struggling for self respect. In categories of sexual offences, women are subjected to acute trauma of rape. In spite of year's hard struggle by women's rights groups and landmark Supreme Court's decisions, the conviction rate of rape cases has fallen from 44.2% in 1973 to 26.5% in 2010. There are reasonable apprehensions that the rate of conviction may further fall down in complete disregard to the objectives of gender justice.

I remember, looking to the gravity of rape offences then Home Minister in Atal Behari Vajpayee government intended to come with a proposal in the Parliament to amend the punishment provisions relating to offence of rape and make this offence punishable with death sentence. Enhancement proposal in the quantum of punishment was with the obvious motive to deter the rape offenders. But we must not be surprised to know that stiff opposition to this move came from none other than women's organizations only. The women organizations pleaded that once the punishment for rape is enhanced to death sentence, the women in the society will go absolutely unsafe. Now the offender will commit two offences. First he will rape the women and then he will kill her as well, to destroy the evidence. He would know that both the offences are punishable with death sentence only. The women organizations had reasonable force behind their arguments which finally made the government to withdraw its initiative. Gender justice is a serious issue. Unless the entire society makes a tough move forward with its sincere and honest intentions to give respect to the women they deserve, it would be very difficult for the law alone to deal with the issues of gender justice.

"In spite of year's hard struggle by women's rights groups and landmark Supreme Court's decisions, the conviction rate of rape cases has fallen from 44.2% in 1973 to 26.5% in 2010. There are reasonable apprehensions that the rate of conviction may further fall down in complete disregard to the objectives of gender justice."

7

Why Do People Commit Crime?

To act criminal is a human tendency. When this criminal tendency dominates he commits crime, otherwise, he behaves normal. We come across the situations where the person either commits crime intentionally or otherwise he did not intend to commit crime but he fell victim of the circumstances and crime took place. From time immemorial the system visualizes for a crimeless society. The legal system defines crime and provides for penal provisions so as to deter people from committing crimes but the crimes go unabated. Now the criminals have resorted to more technical means to unleash crimes in the modern society. Despite criminal laws, criminal courts, and punishments, the question remains unanswered as to why do people commit crime?

Every crime is not circumstantial. Criminal gangs organize well planned crimes as professional activity. Off late crime has become a profession now. Old researches revealed that criminals suffer from sick mentality. They used to derive sadistic pleasure out of the pain they caused to others through crimes. But today's well planned professional criminality suggests that the criminals are not sick but they act smarter and more alert than the law enforcement agencies.

Conflict of interests in the society is one of the major causes behind criminal behavior. People have conflict of interests on the grounds of caste, religion, region, language, gender as factors of 'social conflict'. Unless the existing system is able to remove such conflicts or takes serious initiatives to balance the conflicts of interests, it would be impossible for the system to stop crimes in the society. The system fails to balance the conflict of interests because of the bitter truth that it plays 'politics' in removing the conflict of interests honestly, while it develops its own vested interests in precipitating such situations. Therefore, apart from criminal psychology, people do take crimes as profession which has nothing to do with the mental sickness. The professional criminals have devised 'crime fixing' at the cost of the system. In such a scenario, we should not expect that the system would work and the criminal justice is bound to collapse.

"The system fails to balance the conflict of interests because of the bitter truth that it plays "politics" in removing the conflict of interests honestly, while it develops its own vested interests in precipitating such situations."

8

Children Exposed To Labor

You can just imagine about childhood of such children who are passing their childhood practicing child labor. The childhood is very innocent without any sense of responsibility. It is quite natural. Childhood is full of pleasures. If there happens to be any kind of pain, it could be physically borne and is nothing to do with the delicate mind of the child. If the children are seen doing hard work in our society then what the meaning one should make out of it? Obviously doing hard labor is to simply earn their livelihood, to fill their empty stomach. The adults doing hard labor, off course includes fulfillment of their family liabilities but at least such kinds of liability and compulsion for the children doing labor should not be there. May be there is a possibility that their parents, due to some disabilities are incapable to earn the livelihood for such children. Then under such situations the children would have to struggle for earning livelihood for their parents as well, and also to earn to fill their own empty stomach. Then what to talk about their childhood?

If the little children of any society on this earth are seen struggling with labor, just merely for their survival and existence, then it simply means that economic position of that society is hopelessly weak. And that too in a country like India despite sixty seven years after independence if the nation's childhood is forced to go for child labor then we can just imagine that this childhood of today would be the youth of tomorrow's young India. On which strong shoulders would the future of the nation be? There would be unemployment all around. We should talk about unemployment only when we are able to provide proper education to our children and then if we fail to employ them. Our children would be able to go to schools only when they become free from doing child labor for their survival. The children while doing labor and uneducated, when become young they would have bigger empty stomach with increased personal economic necessities. Childhood passed away doing hard labor, there was no occasion for them to go to school for education. Now what would our these youngster do? For fulfillment of their economic necessities? They would be seen some way or the other here and there extorting, robbing people, doing crimes and breaking laws. Then we will pass on comments that our society has become full of crimes, crime rate has been increased. Before putting all blame on such forced youngsters, have we ever thought of those state of affairs and economic weakness and to what extent our political bankruptcy was to be made culpable for all that child labor?

Please, do not make such statements that our present India is getting socio-economically so strong that begging children on the streets and children doing labor are now not seen in our society. Have a talk some time, with such children. You will find that such children are forced to do labor not just for the sake of their empty stomach only but they also bear the responsibility of their poor old parents, brothers and sisters as well, on their shoulders. Now what amount they would be in position to earn by the evening so that it could meet out the expenses of their family? If they are not able to, then other young brothers and sisters would also be forced to leave home and bear the burden of the family. There would not be some fifty or hundred such families in India whose childhood passes away by doing labor. The number of such families must be in lakhs and lakhs. When after all, they would be able to go to schools and educate themselves. There are data of Planning Commission of India that about forty percent people of entire Indian population either live or are forced to live below the poverty line. When such children would be getting rid of poverty then only they would be in a position to think of going to schools? Now they would feel that there is no need to work to support the family. Childhood is the most beautiful feeling of anybody's life. That has just passed away doing child labor. If there is any system on this earth which can bring the childhood of such children back? And can do justice with such children?

Then such children will also be properly educated and would be employed and would not be forced to commit crimes for the sake of their empty stomachs.

There could be scope for suggestions to deal with serious problem like child labor particularly when there are no such provisions in our Constitution and other statutes. But by merely making provisions prohibiting child labor through Constitution and other statutes, the problems are not solved. From where should we bring the sincerity and honesty to enforce these prohibitory provisions? The will power to enforce would come from the inner conscience of the political and executive managers and their positive mindset. The Constitution makes it explicitly clear that economic inequality from the society should be removed. What to talk about reducing economic disparity among people? Let us not talk about data when such pathetic situations are directly seen in our India that too when the Planning Commission admits to it. The circumstances should be perceived through sensitivity and what is needed is that the system managers should make proactive efforts towards strict implementation of the rule of law by making themselves accountable to their inner soul. There are lot many laws for right of the children. The fundamental law of the land itself talks about free education to the children of such weaker sections. But how would they go to schools with hunger in their empty stomachs? They need to be protected not only from hunger but from malnutrition as well. When they feel no compulsion to work, then they go to schools with free mind, educate themselves, and become responsible youth and then make the nation strong. Its humble submission that there should not be mere talks of justice to be delivered to the children but they should be given the real justice too. Please...!!! Their childhood should be restored to them.

"And that too in a country like India despite sixty seven years after independence if the nation's childhood is forced to go for child labor then we can just imagine that this childhood of today would be the youth of tomorrow's young India. On which strong shoulders would the future of the nation be?"

9

Corruption, Corruption and Corruption

Tendency of corruption is now proving to be fatal when we start presuming with a mindset that corruption is now omnipresent and we cannot help. Our mindset itself has conferred a kind of social acceptability to this cancerous corruption. This acceptability has been made to the extent that if a person is serving as public servant in any government job then as a matter of great pride he never forgets to tell others that what a large scope he has for underhand income in his job. We also in the society appear to be very anxious to know from the other person that he must be having a handsome income over and above to his salary. During marriage proposals, the side from the bride has been seen concerned making much more inquiries about the scope of unlawful earnings for the groom rather than his legal remuneration and when possibilities of such scopes are confirmed, they are the happiest persons on this earth to finalize the marriage relationship without further delay. Honesty for a person to be the best policy has now become a matter of gone days. Today for a person being honest is not a character for him, but it is said that a person who is honest must be coward since he has no courage to accept bribes. Because he is coward that is why he is forced to live honest. Doing unlawful acts, violating laws and indulging in corruption is considered to be the job of mighty people and not of the coward honest one. The people who are corrupt, who are breakers of the laws are also mighty one in the sense that despite that entire unlawful act they do, the general impression is that the legal system of the country is helpless to cause any harm to them. And this thing only is linked with their social status, their social acceptability is thus established and the rule of law is sidelined.

Corruption has also its own criminal jurisprudence with its own peculiar criminal psychology behind to commit it. It spreads all around and becomes quite visible for the reasons because such mighty people no longer have any fear of law or punishment in their mind. They are heard saying that what the most law can do? It can only punish, that too when the offender is proved guilty. They fully know that law of the nation would not be in a position to punish them because they will see to it that the case against them is not proved in the court. Evidences will not be able to reach to the court of law, but would be destroyed. Law would not be in a position to see all that because the law itself is said to be blind. How could it see after all? For the lack of evidences the mighty corrupts one are left scot free by the law and discharged with due honors. Facets of corruption should not be limited to economic corruption only. The facets of social corruption are also very draconian. Our nationalist thinking has been destroyed for centuries due to prevalent tendencies of societal exploitation into the caste system. But law of our country neither could get any way out to avoid this negative approach and get rid of this caste based social disorganization till now, nor there appears to be any such serious initiative in the near future.

The instances of social corruption are equally heart provoking. If economic position of the parents of a girl is not good, they are poor, they are unable to give dowry as consideration to marriage, then this society will kill the girl by burning her alive on the charges of not bringing dowry. Or the society will go to the extent of torturing the girl and create a situation that one day she herself commits suicide and ends her life. Our so called civilized and educated society will not have even a wrinkle on its face, and social corruption goes on and on. Taking bribe and giving bribe amounts to be an offence, it will remain so in the statute books only, law will not be in a position to take action against anybody since nobody will come forward with any evidence to help the law of the land.

But we have moved so forward in the chain of social corruption that its credit must go to the science and technology. A situation for dowry torture would only arrive at when our girls would be allowed to born alive. We will not let them to take birth and ensure to kill them in the fetus of the mother itself. The matters relating to killing of female fetus has become a very normal thing in the modern society. There are legal provisions in our legal system for preventing such crimes and punishing such criminals, but they have completely lost their affectivity. However, in true sense before blaming the legal system we as members of society need to bring a change in our mindset and our conduct. See...!!!... Law is not in a position to perform its function because our own conduct is not up to the mark. Our conduct has become corrupted not only to the extent of committing crimes, but there after too we ensure that all the evidences are completely destroyed. Our corrupt conduct makes the entire legal system completely impotent. Remember...!!! Impotency of the system could never give birth to justice.

"Our conduct has become corrupted not only to the extent of committing crimes but there after too, we ensure that all the evidences are completely destroyed. Our corrupt conduct makes the entire legal system completely impotent. Remember!!! Impotency of the system could never give birth to justice."

10

Human Rights Jurisprudence

The jurisprudence relating to human rights is very strange. Strange!!! Yes..!!!... Why not? We talk about human rights too much. We clamor that human rights should be made enforceable under the law. At the same time there are reports of regular violation of human rights in the society. If we happen to conduct a serious study of human rights jurisprudence then we find that these are the rights which have direct link with human existence and its dignity. It is pleaded that since people have taken birth as human beings then at least they should be separated from living with animal existence. What has gone wrong with it? By merely writing them into human rights documents and keep on clamoring for them as human rights would be of no use, unless we are able to administer the droplets of human rights to the people. Nothing could be easier than shedding crocodile tears and talking endlessly on human rights, as if we are so obliging to the poor human beings? At international levels Universal Declaration on Human Rights are made in the year 1948. That all human rights are quite significant and natural for human life so that with the help of these human rights people can live their life with human dignity.

Today the conditions of hunger and poverty are so aggravated all around the world that there appears no need to comment on it. Barring few rich countries, if we talk about human dignity for the people living in poor countries, it amounts to more than cheating. Let them get rid of malnutrition, starvation should be abolished and at least with minimum levels of living conditions then only we may talk about their human existence. But the reality is that probably by the time planning efforts are made by the system managers for affording human dignity to them, their life starts coming to an end. The bare talks of human rights are left behind on this earth only again to continue talking about the human rights of next generations. It goes like that only and such rights are getting buried with the dead body of the person. Now it has become the destiny of majority of people to remain on poverty line, then move down below the poverty line, further below and below. We talk of destiny as an excuse, particularly to conceal our drawbacks. When destiny itself does not admit to it, we will keep on making wasteful efforts just for the sake of it and will continue talking about human rights as a fashion of the day. When we have declared that we shall see to it that people are conferred with their basic human rights, then what goes wrong within the system that the people are denied of these rights?

A very interesting jurisprudential fact is that unless human rights are incorporated under law by means of an enactment by a competent legislature, human rights do not acquire statutory status. We will keep on talking for human rights but they would not be enforceable by law and the people would have to be dependent on the mercy of the system only to get these rights. When many of such human rights have not been given the status of a legal right, then how the legal system would be in a position to help out the people in enforcing such rights. Thus under such circumstances people live at the mercy of the system only and are unable to make any claim as a matter of right. Then where is the right? The mercy of the system we are witnessing since long. Poverty, hunger, malnutrition, ill health, lack of education and life of the people even worse than animals all around. We need no evidence for it.

If we are going to blame the system then you will say that my thinking and approach is quite negative but at the same time there is nothing worth positive to say about all that. If something is there it's merely tip of the iceberg. If the talks about human rights remain limited within the charters and documents only and that every human right does not get the status of a legal right then under no circumstances talks about justice or injustice would itself be of any meaning. What to talk about the enforcement of such rights? Yes…!!! Off course it is quite strange.

"Thus under such circumstances people live at the mercy of the system only and are unable to make any claim as a matter of right. Then where is the right? The mercy of the system we are witnessing since long. Poverty, hunger, malnutrition, ill health, lack of education and life of the people even worse than animals all around. We need no evidence for it."

11

Education Commercialized

Let us accept this bitter truth that due to lack of the political will the basic education has been collapsed. Government planners have completely failed to ensure honest implementation of basic education policies in their true letters and spirit at grass root levels. The planners should not take the excuse that they only plan the things, and its enforcement is not theirs job. Regularly reducing number of children in government owned primary schools is indicative to the fact of deteriorating basic education whether in rural or urban areas. The most shocking fact is that although a good number of teachers are appointed in these primary schools but they never bother to go to schools regularly, attend to the children and contain the decreasing number of students.

Such prevalent state of affairs has given rise to mushrooming growth of privately owned public and other convent schools, not only in urban areas but in rural areas also. Such schools are functioning purely on commercial basis, without having any quality control on part of the government. The privately owned mushrooming growth of public schools has completely commercialized the education, by taking undue advantage of absolute carelessness on part of the caretakers of the education policy.

This deteriorating scenario is seen not only in the fields of primary education but in secondary education as well, where government owned highs schools and intermediate schools are struggling very hard to survive against the onslaught of purely commercialized private schools. The government schools are almost on the verge of collapse. The dreaded tentacles of commercialized education are also engulfing within itself the fields of higher education too. In recent times we are witnessing a sharp growth of universities owned by the private sector.

Paying price for a good quality education is not bad. But in a country like India this factor could also not be ignored that as to how much population in India is economically capable to afford the expensive primary, secondary or higher education in such privately owned educational institutions? The Constitution of India talks about affording equality of opportunity to every person as far as his social, economical and educational advancement is concerned. There are people in Indian society who cannot afford equality of opportunity through these schools due to their weak social background and poor economic conditions. Should we not consider it as responsible citizens of this nation that prevalence of such unequal situations in education policy of our country is totally against the spirit of the Indian Constitution? We the people of India need to think about educational justice to be kept in association with justice- social, economical and political.

"Regularly reducing number of children in government owned primary schools is indicative to the fact of deteriorating basic education whether in rural or urban areas. The most shocking fact is that although a good number of teachers are appointed in these primary schools but they never bother to go to schools regularly, attend to the children and contain the decreasing number of students."

12

Socialist Considerations under Constitution

What do we mean by socialism in literal sense? A thought, a policy initiative which should be for upliftment of society, treating every person to be equal. A concern for the society, for betterment of the society as a whole considering to the fact that, "every person is born equal on this earth", to afford every person an equality of opportunity in all aspects of society so that they are also equally benefited from the natural and state resources.

As distinct from capitalistic and communistic approach the socialism endeavors to provide an environment which must be conducive to exploit the amenities at grass root levels in the larger interest of the masses. But the big question is whether as on today, our state administration is in a position to exploit the situations or to afford the opportunities for the sake of protecting social and economic interests of a big majority of Indian population? Better economics is the basic interest which needs to be protected as a top priority. Do we remember any economic policy which is for the masses and is completely free from corruption on part of the public authorities? Perhaps none...!!!

That's right. We have ensured mixed economic structure as central philosophy of socialism, where there will be a healthy co-existence of public sector and private sector both. Even the smallest of the business entrepreneur, who has the vision and the business acumen to pursue with, he will have the business environment provided by the legal mechanism of the country. He will have the fundamental freedom of trade and commence of his choice in any part of the country subject to certain reasonable restrictions.

Equality of opportunity in a country with socialistic bent of mind is absolutely denied, when there are allegations of the nature that the economic policies of the country are being framed by the governments under the influence of big industrialists. They are reported to commonly interfering with the decision making processes just to protect their own immediate business and economic interests. The governments usually oblige them for vested political reasons. This is absolutely unfair and unjust. If the economic policies will be formulated by the governments to show undue favors only to big industrialists, then it amounts to mockery of socialism. Let the people of India forget about what they actually mean by socialism? Yes…!!! It sounds good only in the books and slogans.

"Equality of opportunity in a country with socialistic bent of mind is absolutely denied, when there are allegations of the nature that the economic policies of the country are being framed by the governments under the influence of big industrialists. They are reported to commonly interfering with the decision making processes just to protect their own immediate business and economic interests."

13

Right to Education

Education is the back bone of any civilized society. Educating people means, educating society for overall development of human civilizations. Education is also to be linked with profession. The purpose to educate is to enable a person to distinguish between, what is right and what is wrong? As to what is just and fair? What one should do and what one should not?

If there is something wrong in the social situations it means that definitely there is something wrong with the education system of that society. Indian society is suffering from acute crisis with the education system in the country. Basic education starts with the learning process of a child. Every child is unique but due to defective education policy at ground level, we are not able to exploit the psychology of a child for his betterment and for the ultimate development of society. Where the backbone of a child is broken by dismal basic education policy initiatives, it amounts to be a curse on the system managers. How the child would be in a position to stand straight with confidence on his feet with his backbone broken one? Government owned primary and municipality schools in rural and urban areas are dangerously careless. They do not know about their fundamental duty to educate our children properly. Even if they happen to know, they are least bothered about it. Because they know it fully well that the political masters are also equally careless in getting the things right. India goes like this only. The right to education has been left buried within jurisprudential premises itself. Jurisprudence is a mere philosophy of law and it has nothing to do with virtual enforcement of legal rights. Making of a legal right and its due implementation are two different things. It should be taken as an honest warning by the caretakers of the system that our innocent children are being brutally denied from their right to education. Mere appointment of teachers in these primary schools has not made any substantial difference. The body language of our children does not speak well and it reveals the entire truth about the kind of right of education they are being conferred with. This grave carelessness of the system is being very cleverly encashed by the traders of education. Once the education is projected as trading commodity then only those can buy it that have purchasing capacity. Purchasing commodities is by choice and by capacity, and not as a matter of right. Private schools are spread all around purely for commercial gain.

Right to education and right to free education to the children of weaker sections of society are confusing. In an era in which education is being sold as commodity, one would have no difficulty to understand as to the quality of education which has been proposed by the system to be free. Poor quality of education would breed poor citizen only. Who is to be blamed? We should not look for excuses and should dare to face the challenge. Majority of people in India are incapable to bear the expenses in public schools. It is a genuine common perception that any commodity which is given free would be devoid of quality. So is the perception with the right to free education. The quality of free education would be hopeless. Or else! Let the system prove this perception to be wrong. Let the body language of our children speak louder about the quality they are getting. System managers can do it but only with an honest and unfailing determination for years and years.

India lacks uniform basic education policy in the country since independence for the reasons better known to the system managers. There exists a virtual division between public schools and government owned schools. Children from weaker sections of the society are denied good education due to inequality of opportunity for economic reasons. This is in complete disregard to the constitutional spirit and defeats the objectives of educational justice. Right to education as a fundamental right should have been incorporated in the Constitution, right at the time of its inception itself. Educational justice should have been incorporated in the preamble, making it to be a basic structure of the Constitution. One fails to understand the moral or social constraints behind it for non inclusion of right to education within the fundamental rights chapter, at the time of making of the Constitution. It has been only in the year 2002 that our Parliament could feel like introducing the Article 21-A by way of Constitutional amendment guarantying right to education to its citizen as a fundamental right. But one feels sorry to say that all is not well in India. You can well understand the very importance of education for proper mental, physical and social growth in a given civilization. We just cannot dare to ignore education to our children so poorly and hopelessly. To whom to blame for, when our supposedly responsible constitutional bodies themselves act grossly irresponsible. You should not be surprised to know that it took a long seven years for our Parliament to enact a law for conferring statutory shape to the right to education. The Right to Education Act was legislated only in the year 2009. We do not wish to know about the factors justifying the long unreasonable delay behind this most important enactment. But at least we can make our humble submission to the system caretakers for an honest enforcement of this right in its true letters and spirit. I am sure that system must be aware of this fact that even today, after long twelve years of its incorporation as one of the fundamental rights, the children from weaker sections of the society are not being permitted access to privately run public and convent schools. Today modern India badly needs educational justice to be delivered for the sake of common man and off course in the wider interest of social and economic justice. We can do it. It is possible, but to be handled mercilessly with a tough hand.

> *"Right to education as a fundamental right should have been incorporated in the Constitution, right at the time of its inception itself. Educational justice should have been incorporated in the preamble, making it to be a basic structure of the Constitution. One fails to understand the moral or social constraints behind it for non inclusion of right to education within the fundamental rights chapter, at the time of making of the Constitution"*

14

Miscarriage of Social Justice

The system has a very broad and varied concept of social justice. Even ensuring justice to the man who is standing at the bottom end of the social fabric. Who is responsible for designing the social fabric? Off course, it is "we the people". Where is the society, which we call to be an equalitarian society? We always clamor for equality? We have made all related provisions within our Constitution which are based upon the concept of equality and no discrimination. Who are equals? And equality among whom?

Let us limit ourselves only to the extent that the system managers facilitate such social situations, which ensure fulfillment of at least basic minimum requirements of the people in the society. They could get sufficient food to satisfy their appetite and of their family members, a shelter to live in and clothes to cover their bodies. Yes…!!! We know that this is a situation broadly due to the fact that there is an economic disparity and economic inequality in the society. It is very painful that majority of people in the society go without proper food, no proper shelter, living absolutely in abundantly animal like unhygienic conditions. Some times their life is even worse than animals. Why the system has failed to provide them to live with human dignity.

There are different dimensions of social inequality. Who is responsible for perpetual social inequality? Despite repeated hue and cry to remove social inequality, why the system has failed so far? Or else..!!! Do we conclude that despite knowing all the facts fully well the system appears to be least concerned about? Yes..!!! The state of affairs prevalent in the society is indicative of gross criminal negligence on part of the system. Lack of food, scarcity of food, malnutrition, starvation deaths, children dying of hunger, unhygienic living conditions, unnatural deaths due to lack of proper medical treatment, absolute failure of the state machinery to provide the basic minimum necessities are the crying situations of gross social injustice. These are not only the negative aspects but the bitter truths of present advancing society, where the components of social justice initiatives have completely proved to be abortive and miscarried.

> *"Or else..!!! Do we conclude that despite knowing all the facts fully well the system appears to be least concerned about? Yes..!!! The state of affairs prevalent in the society is indicative of gross criminal negligence on part of the system."*

15

Where is the Rule of Law?

A.V. Dicey has talked a lot about the rule of law? Rule of law has to prevail over all priorities and makes it absolutely clear that there would be no discrimination. Every person will be equal before law and every person will get equal protection of laws. Constitutions of various countries which believe in rule of law have made adequate provisions in their statutory regime as right to equality to be a fundamental right. But the most painful question which usually comes to my mind that, whether there is a rule of law in true sense? Do we think that by merely putting the concept of rule of law in law books, we become rest assure that rule of law has been established? My humble submission is that theoretically incorporating rule of law is totally different then by practically assuring rule of law.

In our so called well developed and well advanced society, there are people who are socially and economically strong enough to get the full advantage of rule of law, or whenever there appears that rule of law is creating any problem to them then they never hesitate to manipulate the rule of law to their advantage. Our present social system has allowed developing a category of "privileged elite class" who are politically and socio-economically so powerful that the rule of law has no meaning for them. They will twist the law according to their own sweet will they like to. On the other hand in the same society there is a "deprived class", who are in majority in number, but they are neither socially nor economically capable, they do not have access to the rule of law therefore, they are denied of equality before law and equal protection from laws. See..!!! It is in no way just and fair that theoretically, they are equal in the eyes of law but when it comes to the plank of reality then it is seen that the system does not make any sincere effort to ensure them an equal accessibility to the legal machinery.

The people who are socially weak, the people who are economically weak and above all the people who are educationally weak, can they think of justice? They do not know the ABC of the law and their legal rights. In case their legal rights are violated like daily earners or labor community, are they financially in a position to fight for their rights in the courts of law? There are people still weaker living below the poverty line. They do not have enough resources even to survive. Admittedly the system provides for legal aid. Honestly speaking how many of them are able to get the legal aid? They will not be able to get the equal protection of laws because of their poor socio-economic conditions. Rule of law will fail to provide justice to them since they are not able to reach to it. We need to redefine as to what amounts to 'equality before law'? Let the rule of law prevail and the poor get justice.

> *"Do we think that by merely putting the concept of rule of law in law books, we become rest assure that rule of law has been established? My humble submission is that theoretically incorporating rule of law is totally different then by practically assuring rule of law."*

16

Knocks Economic Imperialism

We misunderstand the industrialization progress to be as advancement towards all inclusive economic growth of the nation. India has its own history of industrialization right from the impact of industrial revolution to the present era of liberalization, privatization and globalization (L.P.G.). The mixed economic system we have facilitates a healthy co-existence of public sector and private sector. Let us not forget that Japan was completely ruined after the nuclear holocaust but in modern global economics Japan is a force to reckon with. Need not to say that it is all due to the great contribution of industrial growth of Japan in recent past. The painful question is as to why the same is not true in case of India?

India has a rich heritage of indigenous small scale and cottage industries which used to strengthen rural India and its prosperity. Global industrial trends made its impact on Indian economic scenario. End of the British rule and post-independence era witnessed a proactive industrial policy, so as to keep in pace with the international industrial advancement. In a bid to keep pace with the global standards, India started completely ignoring its rural economics. The obvious result was that the cottage and small scale industries came to stand still and ultimately ruined. We failed in maintaining the traditional rural- urban balancing of economic structure. We were very much in hurry to adopt the industrialization process without any concrete measures to keep supporting rural based small scale industries till the Indian socio-economics was ready for constructive transition. Industrialization too was not uniform and suffered from lack of proper planning. It restricted to metros and few other big cities only which gave rise to an unparallel rush of people from rural and small cities to these places in search of employment. Due to this defective economic planning even after these much years of independence we are not in a position to claim that we are a powerful industrial nation. Before we could be an industrial force with all half- hearted preparedness, India was forced by international economic imperialistic tendencies to enter into an era of L.P.G. and open up its markets for rest of the world.

Let us admit this very fact honestly that India is under pressure from International Monetary Fund (I.M.F.) and World Trade Organization (W.T.O.) and has already invited economic imperialism to rule on its soil. This imperialism has started stretching its tentacles to engulf within itself the Indian economic prosperity. We would welcome L.P.G. but not at the cost of our own indigenous economics and without restructuring our rural- urban economic structure. The masses in India are facing poverty due to destruction of indigenous economics. Indian rural- urban economic health is unsound and needs to be given proper uniform treatment to make India economically sound. First we must set our home right for an all inclusive economic prosperity than we should think of inviting the world at large. Why do we tend to forget that charity begins at home? We urgently need to support our rural-urban base to become a strong nation.

"In a bid to keep pace with the global standards, India started completely ignoring its rural economics. The obvious result was that the cottage and small scale industries came to stand still and ultimately ruined."

17

Mercy Petitions

Imposing death sentence became a debatable issue now-a-days particularly under the circumstances when the Government of India sprang into action with a series of hangings one after the other. The executions were done after the President rejected their mercy petitions, after a prolonged pendency of years of state of indecision at the hands of the system.

Mercy petitions are filed as a last resort to escape death sentence. It should be noted that at this stage right from the trial court to the apex court of the country endorse death sentence to the accused keeping in mind the evidences, nature and severity of the offence. The concept of "rarest of the rare" cases is in practice, as a ruling guideline of the apex court, to be taken into consideration by the trial courts, while awarding death sentence. According to the Supreme Court *modus operandi* of the crime being inhuman, cruel, barbarous, brutal, intentional human killings would be the rarest of the rare situations to justify death sentence. If the facts and circumstances of the case so reveal such cruelty and brutality of the crime, the trial judge can without any hesitation award death sentence after recording the reasons into writing. Awarding death sentence and its confirmation by the appellate courts, after examining the questions of law, is purely a judicial action, whereas its execution thereafter, is an administrative action.

As the name itself indicates, the mercy petitions have no scope for judicial scrutiny, because after passing through rigorous process of three tier judicial hierarchy, the criminal justice system is satisfied that the accused is found guilty and he should be hanged. Now it is the mercy only which may commute his death sentence into life imprisonment for justifiable reasons or else his mercy petition may be rejected. The Constitutional provisions does not provide for any specific time limit within which the mercy petitions should be disposed off, either this way or that. Obviously, it is expected that within a reasonable time frame the system should take a decision. We should take notice of the fact that this uncertainty may give rise to misuse of the process of law. We all know that delay defeats the ends of justice. For the reasons best known to the system, the mercy petitions are kept pending for years altogether and no decision is taken. Political manipulators start taking undue advantage of the state of indecision. When the judicial system of the country has done its job perfectly, now one fails to understand as to what prevents the administrative system to take a decision promptly and allow the matter to be delayed unnecessarily without any sufficient reason. For the state of indecision on part of the system the offenders found guilty remain under a mental trauma of hanging for years and years. This is inhuman and provides a good ground to human rights organizations to criticize and oppose such considerably delayed executions. Further starts a series of litigation in the form of petitions before the apex court. In a number of judicial pronouncements the Supreme Court has held that delay in execution of death sentence without any justifiable reason becomes a genuine plea for admitting such petitions. On humanitarian considerations the Supreme Court converts the death sentence into life imprisonment. It is an admitted fact that mercy petitions remain pending for decades. There are petitions before the Supreme Court with prayers that petitioner's death sentence should be commuted to life imprisonment. This is not good to see that long unreasonable pendency due to administrative inaction will be under scanner before the Supreme Court and would become a ground for the serious offenders to escape death sentence. The same Supreme Court which had confirmed the death sentence finally would have to sit again to 'review' its own verdict, for the laxity on part of the executors. This is a message not good enough for the administrators of criminal justice system.

No doubt execution of death sentence is painful that's why it is inhuman. Abolition of death sentence needs thorough consideration but never at the cost of social security. India being a democratic country, confronts across the debates between the groups of pro and anti death sentence. Keeping in mind the recommendations of Law Commission of India, death sentence is to be retained in law books but the quantum of awarding death sentence has been reduced considerably to minimum in 'rarest of the rare' cases only. Celebrating some body's death is not in keeping with established norms of civilizations. But like in Delhi rape case we came across an aggressive popular demand to hang the culprits accused of rape, we can understand the dilemma of the system, which has been 'sandwiched' between the two contradictory demands. But the system needs to come out of this dilemma, particularly while deciding mercy petitions and take a prompt decision into these petitions which appear to be worth considering on the grounds of mercy. Otherwise objections would be raised and system would have to face criticism, for the matters kept pending for decades, only to be rejected all of the sudden. Now the system springs into action to execute it. Well…if it was to be executed only this decision could have been taken reasonably right at an early stage itself and the accused could have been saved from the acute mental torture for all these years of pendency. Whether there came up any fresh ground during all these years which became instrumental in rejecting the mercy petition? If no… then it would have been rejected well within a reasonable time limit. It is inhuman. Either execute it or leave it. No dilemma. Otherwise judicial system is left with no option but to step in and do the justice as deemed fit under the circumstances.

"No doubt execution of death sentence is painful that's why it is inhuman. Abolition of death sentence needs thorough consideration but never at the cost of social security."

18

Imprisonment for Life

Life imprisonment is one of the statutory corporal punishments provided under the penal statute books. Imprisonment represents preventive theory of punishment under penal justice system. The purpose is that the convicted offenders should be kept in prisons away from the society. It is also to be kept in mind that by keeping criminals behind the bars the justice system prevents them from repeating crimes in the society and it is also significant from view point of social security.

Imprisonment means the term to undergo punishment in jails for the duration so provided by the competent court in order of conviction. It should be in due conformity within the range of imprisonment determined by the legislature. The competent court can apply its judicious discretion within that range. In recent times there are debates over the term of life imprisonment. What does the life imprisonment mean? Whether it is for a term of 14 years, 20 years or for whole life, till the prisoner dies his natural death while undergoing imprisonment. There is no ambiguity about it that life imprisonment means imprisonment for life. On number of occasions the apex court has also made it expressly clear, that the convict has to pass his whole life behind the bars. Confusion crops up when the appropriate governments use their statutory discretion arbitrarily and release the life convicts earlier on pick and choose basis. However, such convicts should not be released having completed less than 14 years of imprisonment.

The purpose behind such provision is that where a convict has already undergone such a length of imprisonment than either on humanitarian grounds or due to reformation in his conduct, he could be released from prison instead of keeping him behind the bars for whole life. A life convict cannot claim it as a matter of right to be released earlier. If for the reasons to be recorded into writing the appropriate government so decides, then it has to apply its judicious discretion keeping in mind the facts and circumstances of the case and also the fact that the life convict so released would not misuse it and would not repeat crime in the society. Maintenance of social security should be the controlling parameter behind every such release of life convicts.

Life imprisonment is awarded for most heinous crimes. There is death sentence for the offence of murder but in the regime of reformatory theory of punishment the execution of death sentence are very rare now and generally death sentence is commuted to life imprisonment either by appellate court or through mercy petitions. Offence of rape too is made punishable with life imprisonment particularly after barbarous Delhi rape case. The infliction of life imprisonment should serve the purpose to deal with hardened habitual offenders and professional criminals. The purpose of the justice system would be defeated if the repeaters of crime are released from life imprisonment by the executive. The justice system should endeavor and deal tough in punishing criminals according to the gravity of the offence and at the same time tendency of the offender towards reformation and his rehabilitation in the society should be very cautiously taken care of.

"The infliction of life imprisonment should serve the purpose to deal with hardened habitual offenders and professional criminals. The purpose of the justice system would be defeated if the repeaters of crime are released from life imprisonment by the executive."

19

We the People

If 'we the people' too look across to our inner conscience then some of the things would be clearly visible, as to what the kind of role we are supposed to play in justice administration of the country and do we able to justify it? The society is made up of 'we the people' and if today we feel that all is not going well then virtually 'we the people' just cannot escape from our liability. As to why did we not bother that everything should go well in the country?

Whatever the laws are there in the society they do not come from heavens. 'We the people' only sit together and make laws for ourselves. There would be a system in which our elected representatives will participate in law making process. Or else there would emerge a dictator from amongst we the people and will impose his fanaticism on 'we the people'. He would precipitate the legal system and 'we the people' would appear helpless in front of him. In today's date let us accept this fact that in some of the world countries there are impact of dictatorial tendencies, may be lesser in number. In the modern well informed world also dictatorial systems are in practice. *John Austin*, who has been a famous jurist, said that law is the 'command of sovereign'. Now the question will arrive whether who in fact should be considered to be a sovereign? Then command is command after all. Means if the command has been issued by a sovereign authority, then the spirit behind it is that such command should be obeyed. Despite the fact that the command may appear to be 'not right' there should not be any scope for opposition to the command of the sovereign. Oh..! No..! This is not the way? Oh..! Yes..! This is the way. The point is that the person who came from amongst 'we the people' only, derives his strength from us under the pretext of providing leadership to us and becomes a dictator ultimately? And now when he has become dictator, he will start passing on his 'commands'. In the situations of violation of such commands by 'we the people', we would have to face the music. We the people would not be in a position to stop such dictating commands. Then off course, 'we the people' start looking into our own inner self and think, whether who is accountable for all such state of affairs? By that time perhaps, it might become too late.

When 'we the people' drafted our own Constitution then always the presumption is that our nation would have a democratic set up of governance and under this system 'we the people' authorize our own elected representatives that they should play their active role in law making process of the country as our elected representatives. 'We the people' in fact are the sovereign. If by electing them as our representatives, we delegate our authority to them to make laws in the Parliament, then we can also withdraw from them of this authority to make laws? If we can elect them as our representatives then we can ask them also that now they are no more our representatives. Whether in our constitutional system such an occasion has arrived at any point of time that any law of the nation came out of our own command as sovereign, we the people? Or…Else if still such a situation arrives at, it should be constitutionally permissible? Whatever the right to legislate, we delegate to our representatives, can't we get a law to show them the door, in the event they fail to perform or perform badly. If not, then it is a big question on our credibility of being sovereign. What do we mean by the constitutionality of such system, where 'we the people' have the right to elect our representatives to the legislative bodies, but when they go corrupt, commit breach of trust or start showing dictatorial tendencies, then 'we the people' have no right to immediately call them back? In these situations 'we the people' of being sovereign is of no meaning.

'We the people' would only be strengthened when our sovereignty is not merely symbolic. Our members of Parliament and the state legislative assemblies are public servants only, they should bother about and serve 'we the people' as their sovereign. And when the sovereign feels like that the services of particular public servant representatives now are no more required then at least the sovereign should be in a position to act like a master and get them out. But in fact what happens is all just opposite to it. The representatives of 'we the people' become so out of control that they even start bargaining for their own sovereign. Once they are elected they will see to it that they complete their full term. We the people are left behind cheated. 'We the people' are sovereign only for the days when the general elections are round the corner and the moment 'we the people' cast their vote, they cease to be what they are supposed to be. Now our representatives will look like sovereigns, grab the ruling power at our strength, show on 'we the people' only the hitting spree of power. If for justifiable reasons 'we the people' happen to argue with them, the representatives would order for initiating legal action against 'we the people' and show the 'sovereigns' the doors behind the bars. However, there is no fun to talk about, as to what is just or unjust, but whenever they feel like on occasions they will just go for asking well being of 'we the people' with crocodile tears for the reasons they target for the next general elections. But the tragedy is that 'we the people' have tendency to forget about all that and again get them to be our representatives. Democratic governance goes like this only to repeat knowingly the same mistake and to choose between the two evils, let that be the lesser one.

"We the people' would only be strengthened when our sovereignty is not merely symbolic. Our members of Parliament and the state legislative assemblies are public servants only, they should bother about and serve 'we the people' as their sovereign. And when the sovereign feels like that the services of particular public servant representatives now are no more required then at least the sovereign should be in a position to act like a master and get them out. But in fact what happens is all just opposite to it."

20

Justice Delivery is not an Easy Task

It is very difficult to define what is justice? And also what amounts to 'delivery of Justice'? In abstract sense, what needs to be done should be just and fair. Now the question may arise whether who will decide that what is just and fair? Or else what could be a standard parameter to measure and say that this is just and fair? If there is 'rule of law' in any existing system and things are strictly operating in accordance with the rules and regulations then it could be said very safely that justness and fairness prevails around. Can the 'rule of law' be the only parameter to ensure justice? Laws and their being 'pious' have a very close and intimate relationship. Can we say with full confidence that where a law is absolutely 'pious', then there is no scope for any discriminatory and arbitrary applications of law? Should we not admit this fact that the moment human agency steps in, either through legislative process or through interpretation of laws, and then the very piousness of laws stand compromised or diluted? Judicial activism would be an exception. How could one avoid involvement of human agency regards execution of laws are concerned? The 'realistic approach' of law must be that right from the level of legislation, enforcement and the interpretation stage of law, its 'piousness' should not be compromised at any stage and that would be the justice in strict sense in its true letters and spirit.

Is it really possible? Isn't it a difficult task? Yes! It is. How to ensure the 'piousness' of the law is not an easy task? Human beings have their own inherent human weakness. Human perceptions towards laws could be different from person to person. Some would have positive perception, while the other would have negative one. Exponents of 'sociological school of jurisprudence' rightly point out that 'conflict of social interests' is the most significant human perception which needs to be controlled and regulated by law. Conflict of interest in society arises out of unfulfilled human greed. Can any law on this earth satisfy or justify the human greed? No..! Certainly not. There are categories of people on this earth in majority, who are not even able to fulfill their basic minimum needs of the day. Whereas, contrast to that there are category of people who have limitless desires to be fulfilled at the cost of the previous category. This is an absolute social injustice, which the world is witnessing as a mute spectator and the justice delivery system is silent about it helplessly.

Till there remain situations of conflict of social interests, economic interests, cultural interests, political interest, castiest interest, regional interests, religious interests, linguistic interests, etc. then merely the constitutional declarations for the sake of social justice, economic justice, and political justice are no guarantee that the justice would be administered in true sense. We provided for the policy initiatives to be made to reduce inequality in income, to remove economic disparity and social disparity and also to minimize concentrations of wealth in few hands. Let us ask honestly from our inner conscience, what the steps we took towards minimizing the gap between the haves and haves not? Even if for the sake of just an eye wash, we do have statutory provisions for the purposes as aforesaid. Do we have the courage to admit this very fact, whether we were able to enforce such provisions in totality? We do have the last hope in our judiciary. I do not think that the judiciary is so helpless to take stock of the situations and the circumstances and fix liability on those who are responsible for this absolute injustice and for their gross violation of duties which they were bound to perform under the law. It appears that the judiciary has met with serious deviations in its bid to establish a balance between the conflicting social, economical and political interests within human perceptions and has failed to achieve its objectives of justice- social, economical and political. Need of the hour is a kind of judicial 'ultra- activism' in its honest perspectives. Or else keep ready for miscarriage of justice.

"It appears that the judiciary has met with serious deviations in its bid to establish a balance between the conflicting social, economical and political interests within human perceptions and has failed to achieve its objectives of justice- social, economical and political. Need of the hour is a kind of judicial 'ultra- activism' in its honest perspectives. Or else keep ready for miscarriage of justice."

21

Regionalist Disintegration

Although India as a nation believes in keeping intact and carrying on the heritage of 'unity in diversity' but still someway and somehow our belief seems to be gets broken and shattered. Yes..! We should have a belief to this fact and feeling that India is one right from Kashmir to Kanya Kumari, but keep protecting this feeling is not easy. First of all let us see whether what do we mean by regional unity? In federal structure of India there is council of states and in political perspectives these states have been conferred with regional autonomy as well, in which administration of the states is to be ensured with through democratically elected governments keeping in conformity with the spirit of the Constitution. The states would have the freedom to maintain their regional identity subject to the condition that such freedom should not in any way encroach upon the comprehensives national structure of India. In our states regional cultural heritage has been imbibed in and our Constitutional sentiments are also dedicated to strengthen such cultural heritages.

It would always be the top priority of any country in the world to keep 'regional unity and integrity' intact. In the Preamble of Indian Constitution it has been categorically mentioned that 'we the people' of India will maintain the 'unity and integrity' of the nation intact. The word 'unity' however, appears to be very simple in listening to and expressing but in true sense in a country like India with full of diversities, maintaining a sustainable unity intact is a very difficult task. I do not understand that in Indian nation we are able to be socially and culturally united. In support of my submission there should not be any need to give any evidence but still I feel equally accountable for my nation India, my aforesaid submissions should be circumstantially corroborated. It should not only be logically confirmed, but the system managers of the nation India, should also ensure solid initiatives towards establishing 'unity and integrity' of the country. People in India do have the feeling in their mind that presently all is not going well in India. We start thinking whether honestly India is one from Kashmir to Kanya Kumari? We come across very disturbing and frightening facts. Separatist tendencies in Kashmir are a serious cause of worry for integrity of nation India. It is not that we would not be able to find a solution for Kashmir problem. But the pertinent question is whether our intentions are clear and not dishonest? The Kashmir problem will continue to be a problem, since we are out to mix 'politics' with it. If the national interest is given top priority then, where is the problem? For last many years regionalist tendencies are witnessed in Maharashtra as well and the national interest is left far behind. A pure 'politics' is clearly seen out there in the entire scenario but still our constitutional institutions are surprisingly feeling compulsions to choose to remain silent. People from Assam are not feeling safe in Karnataka whereas, in Assam people belonging to Bihar are forcibly ousted. Bihar and Jharkhand people have their own regional differences. Whatever the political arguments are being given for the sake of Telangana but voices are raised high in support as well as in opposition. There are pleas and counter pleas to further disintegrate Uttar Pradesh and Bihar so as to create another Bhojpur state. They may not make any effort to know about the sentiments of the people living over there but their political ambitions are loud and clear.

Whatever the options we have, are very sound and clear. There are no two opinions about it that India has been a country of diversities. Our country is known and has its own identity in the form of very diverse beautiful regional cultural heritages. We should always feel proud of it and it's our duty as well, in keeping these regional cultural heritages intact. Do we disintegrate the nation into pieces in the name of regionalism and individual political ambitions? That's right, it's a convincing argument that much part of bigger states does not get socially and economically developed and remain backward. After breaking them into smaller states it will be quite convenient to our political system managers to concentrate for their development and remove backwardness. That's good..! We should think *bonafide* and should not doubt the intentions of our political managers. However, had there not been lack of political will, these smaller parts of the bigger states would not have backward and would have remained in the mainstream of the development.

We should have a very genuine concern that once our states are divided into such small parts and on any such subsequent occasion if so needed in the larger national interest, would we be in a position to bring them back in shape? For the sake of Almighty let us pray that such a situation does not arise. In our families also, when there is a division, one brother starts living separately from the other one and it never sounds good. Somewhere, someway it definitely disintegrates the family interests and weakens the strength of our nation's unity. For centuries our nation has been painful victim of the tendency of 'divide and rule' and has been kept suffering, disintegrating and weakening. If there are honest arguments for development and removing backwardness, then such development should be visible down to the grass root levels. Otherwise regionalist disintegrations would render our nation weak and weak. Right from childhood we are made to understand from forefathers that 'united we stand and divided we fall'.

"People in India do have the feeling in their mind that presently all is not going well in India. We start thinking whether honestly India is one from Kashmir to Kanya Kumari? We come across very disturbing and frightening facts."

22

Democracy Paralyzed

Behind introducing democratic system in India the only intention of the Constitution makers was that after centuries under foreign rule now there should be no scope of aristocracy or autocracy in independent India. Now it has been for the people of India the way they like would ensure social, economic and political administration of the country. The people of India would create such a people's force which would maintain the unity, integrity and sovereignty of the nation intact. People's power does not only mean the 'vote politics' that through general elections the elected governments would take over the possession of the power and start functioning out of control. If democratically elected governments, after a space of time start looking that now they do not appear to be of the people, they do not act for the people, then such governments have no right to continue in power. Our democratic system completely looks paralyzed when such governments despite unwillingness of people remain in power in the name of constitutional compulsion to complete their term.

Our Constitution of the country talks about political justice too. Let political justice also be ensured along with social and economic justice. What do we interpret about political justice in fact? Do we consider that political justice merely means people's freedom to exercise their right to franchise? That's all..!

And that too under the watching guns of Indian paramilitary forces. What kind of justice has in fact been intended in democracy by means of political justice? Does it mean for those who practice politics as their profession? Their political right should be protected in perfect democratic manner and that there should be no encroachment whatsoever to their right to profess politics. Or else is there any scope of 'political justice' for such people also, whose role in this democracy is limited only to the extent of casting their votes?

We are forced to think and should never hesitate to admit about the prevailing state of democracy as an institution. Could we think of the reasons that holding of general election, which are directly linked with the concept of political justice, are impossible without deployment of paramilitary forces? What is going to happen after all, if deployment of paramilitary forces is not done or is withdrawn? Yes..! Sorry we cannot even imagine about it. We take a sigh of relief, when during general elections hundreds of people are killed following election related breaking of law and order. The administration is seen claiming that everything went off peacefully, there was not much bloodshed, some hundreds of people died in electoral clashes. That's it. If according to Abraham Lincoln in a democracy, the government is by the people, of the people and for the people only, then why this bloodshed? Why the shape of democracy has gone so draconian? Why the people's system became so handicapped and weak that it could not even protect its own shape? Democracy is, if by the people and of the people, and if the people themselves could not keep it in its shape and health intact, then to whom should we blame for? If there is degradation of moral values in men, then for such degradation the men themselves are responsible. We should agree to this very fact that in our society there is serious downfall of democratic values and we should look for the reasons not anywhere else but within our democratic system itself.

India is considered to be a big and powerful democratic country in the world. Does it not create a state of confusion in considering a country to be powerful merely by means of counting its big population? We need to be a powerful country in reality. The population of a country could be a force in democratic sense provided people's right of franchise is protected intact with the people, but population of any country could not be any measurement for calculating its social and economic strength. Democratically we may be a powerful country but proportionate to our population we are not that powerful and strong. If countries with small population like England, Japan, Korea are comparatively more powerful countries, then that is on the basis of the strength of their citizen's honesty, dedication, integrity, dutifulness and sense of belongingness for their nation. We, when once elected as people's representative, and then we have the tendency to forget about our sense of accountability towards our electorate and the nation. And instead of transforming our democratic strength into nation's strength, we make it handicapped for the sake of our vested interests in such a manner that our entire democratic values go shattered and destroyed. For fulfilling of personal political gains, we are in the habit of collecting people's mob even for petty reasons and instigate them to commit all loot, arson, bloodshed and destroy public property. It has become a common *modus operandi* for display of power and strength. Instigating people for use of criminal force against each other, destroying property of the nation, fuelling a kind of feeling of ill will and mutual hatred among the people, is going to prove a dangerous tendency for show of political strength. It will vanish healthy socio-economic environment of the nation and needs to be avoided at any cost. In the greater interest of the nation and larger political justice, democracy be saved from being converted into mobocracy.

> *"If democratically elected governments, after a space of time start looking that now they do not appear to be of the people, they do not act for the people, then such governments have no right to continue in power. Our democratic system completely looks paralyzed when such governments despite unwillingness of people remain in power in the name of constitutional compulsion to complete their term."*

23

Capitalistic Tendencies

The moment capitalistic tendencies come in mind, it makes an impression of a system which has been established or strengthens itself by exploiting people without resources, of labor class, weak and poor. Historical facts reveal that 'communism' came into existence as a strong protest to 'capitalism'. In capitalistic system 'power of money' proves to be much heavier over 'man power'. In comparison to money, people appeared to be absolutely powerless and disabled. Let it be any civilization, you just cannot ignore the importance of money. Significance of money could be a relevant fact but difficulty arises when the very human existence is made subject to power of money. There is a majority of population in the entire world, who either do not have sufficient money to fulfill their day to day requirements or forget about sufficient money they are anyhow just limping on and compelled to live their life in utter scarcity.

Democratic system is the 'peoplist system', as a system of the people, by the people and for the people. The very objective of this system was that where the corridor of people's power emerges out from amongst the people only according to their consensus. Where public opinion determines the direction of people's power, control it, conduct it and if the people feel that people's power is deviating from its rightful path then the people's opinion only should set it right to the proper tract. In the larger interest of peoplism the people only should pick up the right alternative so that situation of any deviation does not arise and it could be controlled and regulated effectively.

With the passage of time people's power also could not keep itself untouched from the attraction of the capital. When the corruption reached to its climax then the power seekers were well able to understand that on the strength of the 'power of capital' they will be in a position to even auction out the 'peoplism'. They became successful also in their thinking and purchased out the peoplism itself. Today the peoplism is completely under the clutches of capitalistic tendencies. By mere imagination of 'peoplistic socialism' or by merely incorporating them in nation's Constitution if 'peoplism' could have been established globally then it could have been so easy a task. This world would not have been a tale of struggles and revolutions. Till our motives are not clear or till we have a dishonest intention, nothing is going to happen by simply making provisions of 'peoplist system' in the documents like Constitution. Several such constitutions will keep on coming and would prove to be dismal. Capitalistic tendencies would keep playing their dangerous games and socialistic thoughts would continue to be thrashed out in pieces without being translated into realistic patterns.

The primary elements of capitalistic tendencies, which are quite visible in our society, are that the people be made so weak, educationally and economically, that they could not be in a position to properly stand on their feet. The basic education is made so broken by its spine that children in the society when become young could not be self dependent. The power of the capital remains in the hands of a chosen few and majority of youth remain at the mercy of capital power to fulfill their daily necessities. Peoplism does not guarantee employment to all. Capitalism too will see as per its 'calculations' if a youth is competent enough, then it will think upon giving employment to him. It means that a majority of youth will be seen roaming around struggling in search of employment. In a country like India where almost half of the population is suffering from poverty and about seventy percent of it is living in village areas. In villages the basic infrastructure in primary education has not yet reached, we are forced to forget about proper education, then how about the confidence and self-dependence would be possible among our youth? This is the shape of our 'peoplist system' with its broken back bone. A big 'neo-capitalist' class has emerged on the basis of its capital earned through corrupt practices. The 'capitalistic tendencies' in the emerging neo-capitalist class are probably more dangerous than traditional capitalists. The 'people's power' of the starved and weak one's has been kept mortgaged in the hands of these capitalistic tendencies. Condition is that the peoplism should give the keys of people's power into the hands of these neo-capitalists through general elections and in turn they will 'take care' of their peoplism. Whatever is written in the constitutions is of no meaning.

"A big 'neo-capitalist' class has emerged on the basis of its capital earned through corrupt practices. The 'capitalistic tendencies' in the emerging neo-capitalist class are probably more dangerous than traditional capitalists. The 'people's power' of the starved and weak one's has been kept mortgaged in the hands of these capitalistic tendencies."

24

Visions for a Casteless Society

Dreams are the dreams only. Whether they come out to be true? Let them not be true, let them be shattered. There is nothing wrong in dreaming or keep on dreaming? Dreams are seen through open eyes too. Now it is up to the person as to what extent he is able to put them in action? Dreams may be seen for fulfillment of individual desires. Leaders see dreams for fulfillment of collective good. Dreaming as such is quite an easy process, but translating them into reality is equally complicated process.

I have also seen a dream. Dream of a 'casteless' society, of a 'classless' society. Can an imagination of a casteless society could be a reality? Is it possible to construct a casteless society? Nothing is impossible provided our intentions are true. In an environment of casteless society the feelings of caste discrimination would not crop up in the mind of the people. Because in the society 'differential circumstances' only generate situations of conflict between the people. People belonging to 'capable castes' make an atmosphere of injustice for the reasons of feelings of hatred against people of 'incapable castes'. In a democratic force counting of numbers is considered to be the strength. Counting the numbers of such incapable weak people, they are the majority in numbers. Then where goes their strength? This strength is buried beneath the economic strength of capable ones. It is said that poor ones have no caste.

Poverty does not discriminate on caste lines. Poor is poor only, so do not ask his caste. But still we do ask. How does it make a difference? The poison of caste mentality is deep in our minds. We look very eager also to hand this legacy over to the next generations.

In India caste based feelings have been a very painful history. Possibly through the entire world 'Varna' system has been practiced in India only. Such information is available in encyclopedia Americana. Entire Indian society has been divided into four Varna. The plea has been that this division is done on the basis of the work profession they perform. When there comes a feeling of 'good work' or 'bad work' in the mind, then the group of people considering to be performing 'good work' they start coming in the role of 'capables'. A social system is made with thinking that good work could be performed only by the people belonging to a particular caste and then it is put into traditional social fabric. Now it is for the capables to maintain this tradition strongly in the future years to come. The capables publicly demonstrate their capability over incapables. The weak incapables are those who are considered only to perform bad work. They are put in different castes. Then starts an unending process of social caste system in the categories of 'forward caste', of 'backward caste', and 'low caste' people, and the castes put in 'dalits' and 'tribal' categories. See the tragedy of the system, when it does not appear to be the end of it, then it is thrashed further by dividing it into caste based words like 'other backward classes', 'more backward castes', 'mahadalits'. Such expressions are included in the 'dictionaries' without any shame for the facts whether who is responsible for such increasing backwardness. For that matter the so called 'dalits' and 'backwards' are majority of the Indian population. But their being in majority does not in any way contribute to their strength and capability. By parameters of democracy may be they are in majority by virtue of their numbers, may be they are reckoned to be a democratic force but since they are economically weak and are in low category profession practiced traditionally by low caste people, therefore their majority number is not going to help them out and whatever the 'democratic force' they possess is kept in 'mortgage' in the hands of economically powerful capable castes.

It appears as if in India the caste feelings have come to stay deep in its social system. Visions for a 'casteless society' would probably prove to be a kind of dream remaining unfulfilled. If we look through the Constitution of India then also we would find that its provisions do not at anywhere appear even attempting to abolish the caste system prevalent in Indian society. However, by Article 17, it has been off course provided, that 'untouchability is abolished' and that the State will not discriminate on the basis of 'caste' meaning thereby the caste system would prevail. But efforts would be made constitutionally to ensure that there is no 'caste based discrimination'. In government records they will make columns asking people to provide information relating to the caste and religion they belong. If even then there are caste based discriminations reported in the society and our political leaders by dividing caste system into 'pieces' continued to cash in their vote bank politics and thrash out the society, if a dalit woman as paraded naked by the people in the society, then how the Constitution in fact can help it out? Constitution can only provide a system which it did. Now, if the people do not go by the constitutional provisions it is up to their good will? Why the caretakers of the system silently keep watching flagrant violations of constitutional spirit? What do you mean by 'civilization'? What do you mean by 'humanitarian considerations'? Talking of justice or injustice is, in fact useless, if it is at the cost of human feelings. Incidents of caste based discriminations in modern India are 'inhuman' by any standard.

"If even then there are caste based discriminations reported in the society and our political leaders by dividing caste system into 'pieces' continued to cash in their vote bank politics and thrash out the society, if a dalit woman as paraded naked by the people in the society, then how the Constitution in fact can help it out? Constitution can only provide a system which it did."

25

Locus Standi and Public Interest

The meaning of 'public interest' is understood in comprehensive sense particularly when one talks about 'interest of justice'. The 'interest of justice' in 'public interest' becomes more relevant, where in the country like India 'socio-economic' condition of crores of people is not good. Presently getting justice from court has become very expansive thing. Such crores of people who do not hope to manage bread for the day, how can they be in a position to arrange money to fight for their lawful rights in courts? So, whether such people would not be able to get justice? Public interest is different from an individual interest. The higher courts would admit cases where public interest is involved. But people are poor only individually. Do we mean by that 'socio-economic' conditions of the people could not be covered within the definition of public interest? So would be the ambit of interest of justice.

There is a principle of law in civil procedure that where there are matters of violations of legal rights or any such other matter then only that person could knock the doors of the court whose legal rights happens to be violated. This is known as rule of '*locus standi*'. Literally it means only that person has the 'locus' to bring a case before the court whose legal rights stand infringed. What would be the situation if such person is incapable to bring a court case for the reasons that he has no sufficient money to meet out the court expenses?

Despite the fact that his lawful rights are encroached upon he would not be able to get any legal remedy and would be deprived from justice. May be its quite possible that his legal rights continue to be violated and the law remains a blind 'spectator'. How can the law go to the person for the sake of doing justice when it is supposed to be 'blind' itself? It is for the person aggrieved himself to come to the court of law and seek remedy. This is referred to as opportunity of hearing to be afforded to the individual under the legal system. Now if the individual is able to arrange for the litigation expenses to reach to the court of law, then well and good, otherwise matter ends.

This is the very problem of rule of *'locus standi'*. If any other person comes to the court of law talking about infringement of the legal rights of any other individual, where such individual was unable to come to the court of law due to poverty and illiteracy, the court will not listen to him. The rule of *'locus standi'*, if enforced strictly then position would be that suit brought on behalf of any other individual would be not maintainable. It posed to be a complicated question to the judiciary. Procedurally such petitions were bad. But comparatively more significant question was that whether our judiciary was so helpless that it could not hear such matters merely for the reasons that the petition was not filed by the aggrieved himself but was filed by some other person on humanitarian grounds, having no locus in the case? The judiciary feels realizes and understands well that doing justice is its liability. Not that to just hear the case and dismiss it on the grounds that the petitioner had no 'loci' in filling the petition. The matter in true sense has remained unheard. Let only the aggrieved come to the court of law for the matter to be heard and enable the court to complete its liability to deliver justice. This will not be the way for the justice to be delivered. Make it a point friends.!! that even after sixty seven years of independent India, whatever the fate of illiteracy and poverty is in the country, honestly speaking majority of our countrymen do not know the "a b c" of law. Talking about their awareness towards their legal rights would be just an eye wash.

The practical aspects of Indian judiciary have been a glorious history where we always feel proud of Hon'ble Justice P.N. Bhagwati, Hon'ble Justice Krishna Aiyer and Hon'ble Justice Rang Nath Mishra. These Hon'ble judges took revolutionary initiative in justice administration through 'public interest litigations'. It was felt with deep sensitivity that if a class of society was unable to get its legal rights enforced through courts only due to its poverty and illiteracy, and merely for this reason justice is not done to it, because he was not able to come to the court of law. This amounted to great injustice for the reasons that such people were not able to come to the court of law to seek legal remedy and get justice. One can understand helplessness of the individual but how come the judiciary goes helpless? That to wait for such individuals to come to the court of law with their 'locus' and then think of doing justice to them. See..! the bigger possibility is that they are not going to be literate overnight and their economic conditions too is not going to be better in their life time. Do we conclude then that they could never be in a position to come to the court and get justice? Then why to talk about the 'rule of law'? Why to talk about the 'equality before law' and 'equal protection from laws'? Why to talk about the 'legal right to get justice' if it is made subject to conditions?

The forceful argument of aforementioned pioneer justices for the sake of 'justice delivery' was that the rule of '*locus standi*' was merely a procedural formality and should not in any manner come in the way of judicial process. What has been considered important is that 'justice administration' rather than 'procedural formality' to be given priority. As a matter of exception it was ruled that *locus standi* will not be applicable in the cases relating to public interest. If any individual comes to the court of law with a matter involving public interest, then such cases would be heard and justice would be done to such class of individuals. The judiciary sensibly felt realized that being in the notice of it that people's rights are infringed but if it appeared to be helpless to do justice with them then it amounted to degradation of judicial prestige. By means of the process of *suo motu* cognizance only the concept of 'judicial activism' came to be established. Now without waiting for the cases relating to violation of legal rights of weaker classes the judiciary takes *suo motu* notice of it and ensures justice to such class of people.

It is humbly submitted that there are lot of matters which though do not come within the purview of public interest but these matters after all relate to violations of legal rights of individuals belonging to poor, illiterate, social class. Initiatives need to be made particularly where matters are very sensitive and of grave nature that rule of '*locus standi*' be relaxed in such 'individual interest' matters as well and the judiciary do take *suo motu* cognizance of it, so that majority of people in the society could get benefit of justice in their life time. Possibly it would be a unique world class judicial initiative in itself and the 'justice' would also feel obliged over whelmingly be so delivered in such a grand manner.

It is humbly submitted that there are lot of matters which though do not come within the purview of public interest but these matters after all relate to violations of legal rights of individuals belonging to poor, illiterate, social class. Initiatives need to be made particularly where matters are very sensitive and of grave nature that rule of 'locus standi' be relaxed in such 'individual interest' matters as well and the judiciary do take suo motu cognizance of it, so that majority of people in the society could get benefit of justice in their life time. Possibly it would be a unique world class judicial initiative in itself and the 'justice' would also feel obliged over whelmingly be so delivered in such a grand manner.

26

Reformatory Justice

It happens, a person deviates from his rightful path, but when he realizes his deviation and intends to come back to his rightful path then, what options he should be given? Either he should be left for keep deviating or he may be counseled to come back to his rightful path. If he has been left behind to keep deviating and the system did not help him to come back then he will be lost and would never be able to come back. Such situation of deviation is harmful not only for that individual but it will not be a pleasant thing for social health as well. A person commits crime in the society, kills people, tortures them, and breaks the laws. That is how he deviates. Why the situations of deviation arrive at in the society for an individual? Did we ever do any such analytical study within society, which could make it clear that why people deviate from their right path? Individuals do not behave deviant since birth. There are prevailing social circumstances which create such situations and compel individuals to commit unlawful behavior. Man made societal deviant circumstances are the matters of serious concern today.

In the process of reformatory justice we pay much emphasis in reforming criminals, since consideration is that if a criminal has committed crime, he would have done it either knowingly or would have been compelled by the situations and circumstances to do that. Sometimes circumstances are not within the control of a man and he commits crime. This perception intends to afford an opportunity to the man with an objective that there needs to be resocialisation of the criminal. The society too with a big heart excuses the wrong doings of the man and accepts him in the society, so that his energy is utilized in a positive manner for betterment of the society. To punish the man for his criminal act is not the ultimate objective of a justice system. The methods like probation, parole system, indeterminate sentence, plea bargaining etc. are pillars of the concept of reformatory justice. With the help of these methods the justice system of the country intends to make the criminal realize that OK you have committed crime, though it is not welcome, but still keeping in mind the circumstances of crime, the justice intends to give you an opportunity to reform yourself. Now it is up to you that without wasting such opportunity, if you are able to reform yourself than it is well and good, otherwise deviant behaviors prove to be very painful. Such repeated deviations finally reach to serious consequences and by that time lawful means to reform a man are closed down, being too late. Now the law is left with no option only to punish the man.

A pertinent question is whether what should be our outlook towards reformatory justice? What should be those parameters on which the spirit behind reformatory justice could be established? Look! Reformation straightway relates with humanity. Where the offender repents of his crime and feels guilty of it and tends to reform himself with his inner conscience. During this tendency only to reform himself if the law also offers to help him, he develops a kind of trust for the sake of law and promises deep inside himself not to commit crime again. Then only the things would materialize in their true shape and reformatory justice would be able to prove its worth. Our legal system is also not flawless. Outlook of reformatory justice is not that easy. If it is seen in its completeness then it comes out that criminal mind of every person differs from one individual criminal to the other one. In those circumstances for every criminal any universal reformatory framework cannot be prepared which could fit in each and every case. Every individual criminal would have different reformatory needs and processes. This difference would be for the reasons that crimogenic factors could be different for every individual criminal. Thus what would be fair is that the system should take pains in making psychoanalysis of every criminal individually and then go for their reformative treatment. See! We should remember that criminality is result of sick mentality. Firstly, his sick mind should be given treatment so that he starts thinking normal. Secondly, he should be put to reformation process. It may prove to be a long and tough process but the system needs to take pains and have a big patience to get the desired results of reforming criminals.

Who will take pains to start with individual reformation process for every such criminal? Psychoanalysis of criminal and their treatment is not an easy process. There always remains a possibility that our managers of reformatory justice may lose their patience? It happens like that only when we lose patience and reformation process is left far behind defeating the ends of reformatory justice. Our research makes it clear that although we believe in the concept of reformatory justice but we have failed to enforce it in its true letters and spirit. Why India only? If we look all across the globe then the conclusion would be that we do not witness the positive impact of reformatory justice around. Crimes are committed in the society regularly for one reason or the other. At least some degree of the impact of reformatory justice would have been noticed? But it could not. Crimes became more violent with the passage of time. Criminal tendencies become more terroristic. Terrorism took to such a professional and hardened attitude that now it appears to be unstoppable. Administrators of criminal justice system apparently look quite worried about it. There is always a terror in the mind of people as to when and in what corner of the world there would be a large scale bloodshed giving rise to big loss of life and property. Dangerous suicide squads keep ready for such violence any moment anywhere. Who to and how to make one understand for their reformation? Whether this fearsome situation is due to existing global socio-cultural system? If yes, then the reformatory justice system is destined to be buried.

> *"Thus what would be fair is that the system should take pains in making psychoanalysis of every criminal individually and then go for their reformative treatment. See! We should remember that criminality is result of sick mentality. Firstly, his sick mind should be given treatment so that he starts thinking normal. Secondly, he should be put to reformation process. It may prove to be a long and tough process but the system needs to take pains and have a big patience to get the desired results of reforming criminals."*

27

Whether Reformatory Justice Works?

The existing concept of reformatory justice system is an integral part of jurisprudence relating to protection of human rights. The obvious objective is that an individual with criminal tendency should be reformed and should be brought to the mainstream of society. The other group of the society is of the thinking whether the reformatory justice system would be able to sustain itself at the cost of social security? On one side the offender commits crime while the system looks more worried to reform him than to punish. The system should have to take notice of this fact that as to what extent this system's approach would make a negative impact on mind of victims of the crime? It would become quite natural that people will raise questions about trustworthiness of the legal system. In criminal trials during prosecution proceedings the State is the necessary party to the case. Interests of the victims of crime cannot be ignored. Law and order needs to be maintained so that crimes do not take place in the society. Prevention of crimes in the society is all the liability of the state. In the event of crimes happening and to see that the victims get justice, it becomes state's responsibility that the criminals get sentence in accordance with law. It is for the state to prosecute the accused through criminal trials before the courts and on basis of evidences to assist the courts in convicting the accused. During prosecution proceedings against the accused, in addition to the state, if the victim or his dependents so consider can engage their own counsel to ensure effective prosecution. Leaving aside reformation of the criminal, where the court convicts the accused but sentence awarded to him does not appear to be adequate to the victim, he objects to it even before the prosecution objects, since the victim is the actual sufferer from the crime.

The humane angle of reformation system is very strong but the victim's side too has a genuine complaint that their humane side should not be overlooked at the same time. Whatever the arguments are there in favor and against the reformatory system, what needs to be seen is that whether this system is worth able to achieve its objectives? Whether reformatory system is put to abuse of the process of law? Whether opportunity to reform is available only to those criminals who have strong approach in the system to get favors? And those who have no approach in the system they remain deprived of opportunity to reform. Whether such double standards do not amount to abuse of reformatory system? Without the abuse of process of law such criminals should also get benefits of reformatory system that indeed are in need of reformation. Keeping in mind the facts and circumstances their cases are also very much covered within the statutory framework of reformatory system but they remain deprived of it because they do not have their pairokar in the system.

Principally probation system has been recognized as reformatory process under the law. Basically it is a judicial order and depends purely upon discretion of the court. A criminal cannot claim benefit of probation system as a matter of right. Looking to the facts and circumstances of each and every individual case if in the opinion of the court it appears that the individual in fact became victim of the circumstances to commit crime and if given a chance he would reform himself. By giving reasons into writing and keeping the punishment under suspension, the court may pass orders to release the offender on probation. He is released on probation on conditions of good conduct and would be under the supervision of probation officer. The probation officer would see that the offender has a tendency to reform himself and does not violate the conditions of probation. On definite intervals the probation officer would prepare and submit a report before the court to the effect that the offender is positively responding towards reformation or if the offender violates the terms and conditions of probation or commits any crime during probation then he would mention about such facts in his report. Taking into account the negative report from probation officer the court will cancel the order of probation, impose the suspended sentence and send the offender to jail. Such matters come into light where we come across serious abuse of probation as a reformatory system. The offenders offer temptation to probation officers for procuring a positive report in their favor or even some times they threaten them to get a favorable report by use of force either through money power or muscle power. By means of procuring reports in such a manner finally they succeed in getting their sentence condoned by the court. Keep aside their reformation, they remain involved in committing crimes and when in trouble they abuse the process of law and get scot free. Similar are the abuses observed where prisoners are released on parole under the reformatory system. Though the parolee is kept under the vigilance of parole officer with due instruction that he will not breach the conditions of parole. Parole officer has to make such reporting to the parole board authorities. The possibilities of corrupt practices and use of force are very much present in this system as well.

Now the question arise that if for negative reasons the very objective of reformatory system defeats then what will be the fate of reformatory justice mechanism? Look..! The offender who procured the benefit of reformatory justice system by manipulating the procedure, rest assure he is not going to reform himself. Now the point remains of the offenders who in fact have tendency to reform themselves and they need the support of reformatory system. We urgently require developing such a calculative procedure in which every individual case should be thoroughly examined on factual basis so that individualistic requirements of an offender could be identified separately and benefit of reformatory system could be assured to them in its true spirits. We should not forget that offenders reform themselves and if they develop a strong faith in the system's motives then they prove to be boon for the system and the society as well. We should make an honest initiative in this direction of reformatory justice.

"The humane angle of reformation system is very strong but the victim's side too has a genuine complaint that their humane side should not be overlooked at the same time. Whatever the arguments are there in favor and against the reformatory system,

71

what needs to be seen is that whether this system is worth able to achieve its objectives? Whether reformatory system is put to abuse of the process of law? Whether opportunity to reform is available only to those criminals who have strong approach in the system to get favors? And those who have no approach in the system they remain deprived of opportunity to reform."

28

Striking Out Exploitation

Going on strike could be a debatable issue particularly in the sense as to what extent it should be permitted under the legal system of a country? In a democratic country like India which is in run of a developing nation there happens to be a big number of working class. Strike under labor jurisprudence has been recognized as an important tool in the hands of the workmen against the exploitative tendencies of the industrialist class. The strike is absolutely just and fair under the circumstances where the workers are unlawfully denied from their right to work and also from their right be get paid for the work done.

There is no reason for any class to go on strike if all goes well. It is only when there is something wrong the situation may arise to call for a strike. Strike is a mode for fulfillment of lawful and genuine demands of the workers which they resort to pressurize their employees. Who will strike? Who will demand rightfully? Off course, the one who have been denied wrongfully? Even today the industrialist class has the tendency to maximize its benefits at the cost of the labor of the working class. The position of the unorganized labor is pathetic and much worse. He is ready to sell his labor in the market because he is poor. If he dares to strike out he would lose his job and would be thrown out. He and his kids have no bread to eat. He knows that the day he goes without work it would be a question of life survival for him and his family members. But this does not mean that the system goes inhuman and this should not be the reason for the employer to exploit because he is helpless due to his poverty conditions.

Proceeding on strike should be considered to be absolutely lawful for workers, but not at the cost of larger public interest. There are industries in services sector which render emergency services to the public at large. The working class engaging in performing emergency services day and night for the sake of people, without doubt deserve special consideration. If the managers of the system are not ready to provide special attention for their genuine requirements arising out of any urgent situation then there is every possibility that there will be a sudden system failure and we just cannot deprive them of their right in the name of public interest. Yes..! He will postpone it on, for the sake of public interest with due respect to the rule of law. Then it is for the rule of law now to keep a constant watch over the factors which give rise to such situations and strike it on, before it is too late. It is understood that the rule of law is for public interest but at the same time this should also not be forgotten that there is a public interest involved in the working class too. There should be no need to strikes. Hopefully, let the justice be done to them even before they think for striking out.

"It is understood that the rule of law is for public interest but at the same time this should also not be forgotten that there is a public interest involved in the working class too. There should be no need to strikes. Hopefully, let the justice be done to them even before they think for striking out."

29

The Victims of System

Victims of the system should be distinguished from the victims of crime. Where people with criminal tendencies take undue advantage of the carelessness of the system and commit crime individually. There are instances of collective violence as well, where innocent persons become victim of such violence on a very large scale. Individual cases of murder, rape, kidnapping, abductions etc. are different from the incidents of communal violence and caste based violence, violence based upon regional and linguistic feelings. Recent trends of extreme criminal behavior are being noticed in the form of terrorist's violence all across the world.

Absolute system failure prepares the fertile ground for absolute violent situations in the society. Violence begets violence particularly when the system remains a moot spectator. Political parties are also to be blamed for the system failure in the sense that they are either caste oriented or communal. They are responsible for fueling violence in the name of region and language. In a country like India where there are different regional languages it becomes very easy for the political parties to exploit the popular feelings and create violent situations. The situation becomes much critical when such political parties manage to get power through popular vote and claim to have the democratic license to enforce their disruptive 'political ideologies'. Such tendency among the political power generates system induced violence. It is much more dangerous for the innocent people becoming victim of it on a very large scale. What is shameful is that when a politically motivated system coupled with its ulterior motive victimizes the category of people who politically does not suite to them.

This is severely criminal by all standards. Now the worry is that when such an intentional and politically charged system rules any country then what will happen to its innocent citizens? The conclusion is that an absolute injustice is bound to happen. Under such circumstances the overall responsibility for ensuring justice to the innocent comes on the shoulders of judicial system of the country. It is painful to watch that the judiciary also expresses its helplessness to do justice under such situations. No doubt 'active judiciary' strengthens confidence building among 'we the people' but what further? The Supreme Court warns against 'excessive judicial activism'. It would be very difficult to define the limits of excessive judicial activism. But active judiciary is most needed in the conditions of complete system failures.

When would the justice be done to the innocent victims of the system? Whether the judiciary feels that by coining such concepts it has been absolved from its accountability to administer justice? Judicial system of the country too is an integral part of the existing system. Whether the system would give a reply to it? Whether the judiciary could dare to punish the system? It is understood that these questions would remain unanswered and people will continue to be made victims of the system.

"Such tendency among the political power generates system induced violence. It is much more dangerous for the innocent people becoming victim of it on a very large scale. What is shameful is that when a politically motivated system coupled with its ulterior motive victimizes the category of people who politically does not suite to them."

30

White Collar Criminals

White collar criminals are the people of high social status. They commit white collar crimes by abusing their official position during the course of their occupation. They have a lust for earning money by resorting to unlawful means in the form of demanding and accepting bribes, commissions, accepting unlawful considerations other then legal remunerations, evasion of taxes etc.

Famous American criminologist Edwin H. Sutherland discovered the type of white collar criminality as distinguished from blue collar crimes. Blue collar crimes are traditional crimes like commission of murder, abduction, rape, theft, robbery etc. In Indian perspectives white collar crimes are categorized as socio-economic offences as which directly influence the socio-economic life of a nation. According to Sutherland the tragedy of the system is that when the people who are socio-economically strong and are of high social status start indulging in such crimes, it's shameful. Accepting bribes, commission, unlawful considerations by public servants to show undue favor to somebody by abusing their official position, is all corruption. This all has become a common phenomenon now-a-days among public servants and the people with high social and economic status. Looking to all that, then what to talk about the people who are socio-economically poor and commit crimes becoming victims of social situations and other compelling circumstances. The white collar criminals as politicians, the bureaucrats, the industrialists, other public servants and business men are so influential in the "power galleries" that the law enforcement people go absolutely helpless to nab them. It is only the poor and the weak that face brunt of the laws, beaten black and blue, and thrashed behind the police lock ups.

Following the two world wars the corruption was at its peak in India. To deal with it the central legislature came with Prevention of Corruption Act 1947 followed by Delhi Special Police Establishment Act 1946. Delhi Special Police Establishment (D.S.P.E.) was conferred with ample statutory powers to investigate matters of bribery offences among public servants and other conspirators. With the passage of time D.S.P.E. came to be popularly known as Central Bureau of Investigation (C.B.I., 1962). The C.B.I. was expected to be a neutral body to conduct investigation of the matters of white collar criminality in an independent manner so as to book the culprits to justice after the trial before the special courts established under the Act. But this agency could not escape from allegations of being used as instrumentality of the power in the centre so as to deter the political adversaries. Act of 1947 was replaced by the Act of 1988 with arguments that it would be more effective than the earlier one. But looking to the increasing numbers and gravity of financial scams by the people in "white collars" in yester years it has shattered the aforesaid argument. We come across instances of such criminality among politicians, doctors, advocates, technocrats, educationalists, judges, industrialists and other businessmen. Film stars in the film industry are reported of evading the taxes, small businessmen go for wrongful monetary gains by resorting to selling of adulterated food in the markets. Hoarding, black marketing and profiteering, false insurance claims, banking frauds, bungling in the share markets etc. are very common. The system cannot claim that it is completely unaware of all that. The million dollar question is that 'who' will bell these influential "cats". The answer is 'none' and the white collar criminality is going to stay in the system.

"The white collar criminals as politicians, the bureaucrats, the industrialists, other public servants and business men are so

influential in the "power galleries" that the law enforcement people go absolutely helpless to nab them. It is only the poor and the weak that face brunt of the laws, beaten black and blue, and thrashed behind the police lock ups."

———————————————

31

Equality before Law?

Equality before laws underlies the principle of no discrimination and the legal system also forbids arbitrary application of law. It has been noticed that in quite contradiction to the concept of rule of law, the administrators of the law apply it discriminately on pick and choose basis. Because of this arbitrary attitude of the administrators the very objective behind the concept of equality before law is defeated. Alright, it sounds good that there should be equality before law. It has been further elaborated that the concept in fact talks about equality among equals and inequality among unequal. I fail to understand the very basis behind this elaboration. Well before ensuring the equality before law they have already presumed that there are groups of people existing in the society, who are either equals or unequal. I can understand the dilemma of the system that for the purpose of ensuring the equality before law to all, first to bring unequal within the category of equals. I am sure that lot many people will come forward with their worthless arguments that it is practically impossible to bring unequal in the category of equals. Unless the unequal are brought into the category of equals it is next to impossible to see the equality and the law is absolutely helpless to ensure equality before law, for the reasons that the system knows it fully well that law is totally blind. It cannot help them out. It can only just interpret the laws.

That's all. Even if it dares to open its eyes to examine as to why the unequal are still unequal and as to what prevents to bring unequal into the category of equals? The law will be made blind. That's it. The people with a mind set for *status quo* would not accept this approach of law. Let the law do justice with its open eyes. If it is proverbial that the 'law is blind', then it does not mean that law should also be bent upon to prove itself that it is blind only and not more than that. We would wait for the law to prove itself that it possesses the needed courage to travel beyond the 'proverbial' limitations too.

What has gone wrong behind establishing an equalitarian society? Cannot we look for a society which holds equal rights, equal benefits and equal opportunities to every person? For equal benefits and equality of opportunities to one and all the system need to find out ways and measures with a determined intention to honestly enforce such equal rights. If equal benefits and equal opportunities are denied then off course it amounts to discrimination. Careless and negligent implementation is also a serious kind of discrimination on part of the so called accountable system. What goes wrong if we work for equality social, economical, political and educational? Categorization of equality among equals and inequality among unequal is a clear indication to the fact that there cannot be equality among unequal. Meaning thereby inequality is going to prevail. Defective and biased social, economic and educational policies are responsible for prevalence of inequality in the society. Discriminatory and dishonest implementations of such policies are also one of the decisive factors in this regards. There are forwards and backwards in the society. Unless all are forwards how would there be social equality? There are rich and poor, too rich and too poor, the gap is increasing day by day. Unless all are rich how the law would treat them 'equals' for the purposes of economic equality? Dual education policy which is struggling between schools managed by government sector and the 'public' convent schools totally owned by private sectors. Who will get admission in private schools? Do not say then 'every child is born equal', again putting them inside proverbial limits. Merely by proverbial concepts of equality the system cannot ensure admission for such children in private sector schools. Where goes the equality among equals? Why to forget that every child is born equal? How long the law will continue to be blind? It is the time for the law to open its eyes and see that equals are equal in true legal sense and not conceptual.

"I am sure that lot many people will come forward with their worthless arguments that it is practically impossible to bring unequal in the category of equals. Unless the unequal are brought into the category of equals it is next to impossible to see the equality and the law is absolutely helpless to ensure equality before law, for the reasons that the system knows it fully well that law is totally blind. It cannot help them out. It can only just interpret the laws. That's all."

32

Income Inequality-Poor getting Poorer

The legal system makes a categorical declaration to minimize inequality in income prevalent in the society. It goes to show that the system 'honestly' admits that there exists an economical inequality. It's a Constitutional directive that inequality in income should be minimized and the disparity in income should be reduced. Directive principles are incorporated in the Indian Constitution for framing state policies in this direction. But it appears that for the reasons since the directive principle are not made enforceable by law the state agencies are least bother to care for these principles. Even after sixty seven years of independence we are clamoring for the decades that poor are getting poorer and the caretakers of the system fail to stop it. Shit..! All crocodile tears!!! Damn with it. It is all due to defective policy making and poor policy implementation. The tragedy is that they do know all about it but why don't they admit it? Shameful..!!! I have not heard of any such clamor that rich are getting poor. They are not destined to be, poor policy manipulators. Yes..!!! 'Garibi Hatao' was the slogan few decades back. The 'sound' behind the slogan is loud and clear. We honestly need to see the factors behind it, as to why we failed to achieve these policy initiatives?

If we minutely examine, then in fact after independence, it was all rich *versus* rich and the poor was nowhere in the background. There are reported instances of the fact that the businessmen influencing the governments in policy formulations to benefit them. They will lobby to participate in the economic/business policy making to their favor. It is all for an obvious consideration. Who is there to lobby for the poor? And why should they lobby for the poor? For what considerations? The result was as expected. The poor are not only getting poorer after independence but they have badly gone down the poverty line. Oh..!!! It is pathetic people living on the poverty line. This itself is a curse on the system. Still pathetic is the condition of the poor living down the poverty line. No hope that they will get the food for the day. Their children are starving and starving. They are undernourished. They will die one day because of hunger. They have no money to get bread for their kids. How would they manage for their health and medicine? The 'welfare state' would helplessly keep looking them dying of hunger. Reports say people committing suicide along with entire family members due to poverty conditions. The state cannot claim to have no knowledge of these reports. It is absolutely inhuman.

I should not be mistaken in the sense that I am out to find fault with the existing system. Are you in a position to close your eyes from these bare truths in your society? If not, then how could I? If one need to hammer on the worst parts of the system it does not mean that he is not optimistic. But where the 'silver lining' is so that one could hope for the betterment. Do not tell me to be optimistic just for the sake of being optimistic. I do not want to be. Show me the silver lining. Supreme Court is the watch dog of the Constitution. Watching dogs are expected to bark and keep barking when they observe something wrong with the system and run them down responsible for the wrong. Yes..!!! Poor getting poorer is an absolute wrong on part of the system. Let us join hands to see as to what went wrong that the system miserably failed to minimize the inequality in income despite bonafide intentions of our Constitution makers. Defective policy implementation and corruption all around are the major factors to my understanding which are responsible for system collapse. I will repeat. It's the system and its caretakers making the vicious environment therein which pushes people towards poverty. System just can't escape from its liability if it is not strong enough to handle the system managers. Help us Almighty.

*"If one need to hammer on the worst parts of the system
it does not mean that he is not optimistic. But where the
'silver lining' is so that one could hope for the betterment.
Do not tell me to be optimistic just for the sake of being
optimistic. I do not want to be. Show me the silver lining."*

33

Unemployed Youth

The problem of unemployment in any society is a curse on the national employment policy of the country. Generation of adequate employment opportunities to the youth is function of the State. We find qualified youth without employment. People are seen arguing attributing to problem of unemployment with the problem of increasing population in Indian society. One cannot escape from its pious function to make policy measures to handle with this problem only on the plea that unemployment is a global phenomenon. This is no argument. Yes… A country like U.S.A. also struggles with the acute instances of unemployment but it does not mean that it gives us a kind of excuse that we are helpless to deal with the problem.

Growing unemployment may have varied kinds of implications. Where the unemployed youth are unable to meet out their day to day economic necessities, they may knowingly or ignorantly deviate from their rightful path to wrongful directions. They may become victims of compelling circumstances relating to unemployment and non-fulfillment of their economic requirements. Let the system managers should not forget that protracted unemployment conditions contain the germs for genesis of crime in the society. Acute frustration in unemployment conditions for a youth is a major compelling factor to break the law. Before it is too late, and unemployed youth goes doing something unlawful, he is not to be blamed for all that the policy makers need to device measures to contain increasing trends in unemployment. It is not impossible to search avenues for adequate employment opportunities provided we possess the will power to do it all.

It is very painful when we come across the incidents that a group of five or seven youngsters within the age group of 21 to 25 years are found involved in bank robberies. The investigations may reveal that some of them were M.B.A. pass outs. This could not be the single instance. Before blaming the youth for their wrongful act, the system managers are to be held accountable first, as to why they are failing in providing jobs to the qualified youth? A youth will never be attracted towards committing crimes if his basic minimum day-to-day requirements are fulfilled. A qualified youth should have a right to employment. This would be a big dimension of social and economic justice as enshrined under the Constitution of India provided the system dares to express its will.

"A qualified youth should have a right to employment.
This would be a big dimension of social and economic
justice as enshrined under the Constitution of India provided
the system dares to express its will."

34

Labor Community Starves

What do we mean by starvation? We often come across news reports about people starving to death, people dying of hunger. Labor community is the socio-economically weaker class of the society. Yes..! Labor community starves. World history has been testimony to this fact that labor used to be exploited at the hands of the capitalist class. This gave rise to two distinct blocks as capitalists and communistic ones. By means of democratic standards the labor communities were much larger in number but because of lack of economic strength they had no say of their own in the system. International labor Organization (I.L.O.) came to their rescue. Labor jurisprudence gave them a sigh of relief that they would also have a just and fair place in the system and justice will be done to them.

The philosophy of labor jurisprudence revolves around welfare of the labor class. The system caretakers are very much aware of the fact that what the labor is earning out of his hard labor is not sufficient enough to bring up his family members. Just imagine how he would be managing his expenses relating to food, health, shelter and other necessaries for his family. These are the bare necessities for survival of the human beings. It would not be possible for him to fulfill these requirements on meager amount of his wages. Off course, he would starve his family would starve too. He would have to cut short even his essential expenses for his future savings as well.

The tragedy is that the system is out to exploit him. Trade union activities are recognized in the system with a view to take care of and represent the interest of the labor. Laws of countries confer legal status to establishing such trade unions for the labor class working in industries and factories. One should not be surprised to see the trade union leaders entering into 'deal' with the industrial managers at the cost of the labors interest. This never has been the intention of law. Once labors interest is compromised at the hands of trade union leaders and the industrialists, labor should not expect any justice from them. Historically exploitation has been at the root of industrial management, which was the reason that the world witnessed industrial revolutions.

Despite such revolutions the bitter truth is that the labor has no alternative but to depend upon these industries only and its managers for his livelihood. Ultimately the poor labor is bound to become the prey of the prevailing industrial management situations. The legal system of the country appears to be absolutely helpless to deliver justice to the labor community in its totality, owing to lack of concrete evidence for the dishonest nexus between the industrial managers and the trade unions leaders. Where nation claims to be developing and to be economically prosperous the labor starves at the same time. Let us not ignore this fact as well that our country has a large number of unorganized labors. Where despite jurisprudential umbrella, interests of unorganized labor goes unprotected, we can just imagine then what could be the socio-economic condition of unorganized labors? Yes..! Starvation beyond imaginations.

"Just imagine how he would be managing his expenses relating to food, health, shelter and other necessaries for his family. These are the bare necessities for survival of the human beings. It would not be possible for him to fulfill these requirements on meager amount of his wages. Off course, he would starve his family would starve too. He would have to cut short even his essential expenses for his future savings as well."

35

Political Justice- Hijacked

Before understanding political justice, we need to understand the political system of the country. The Preamble of the Indian Constitution makes it amply clear that political governance in India will be through democracy. India is the biggest democratic country in the world. Famous American President Abraham Lincoln had made it categorical that in democracy the government is of the people, by the people and for the people. The political governance of India is federal in nature. There will be a Union of States with central government to rule the nation with state governments in respective states.

There are Members of Parliament (M.P.) or Members of Legislative Assemblies (M.L.A.) who are the elected representatives of 'we the people of India'. As elected representatives they have to participate in Parliamentary and Assembly proceedings on behalf of the people of India. They represent the public opinion in these legislative bodies and participate in the law making process for the country. Laws are basically the rules and regulations to control and regulate the human behavior in the society. Majority of the people in India either belong to poor class or medium class. The rich class is only handful of such majority. But the reality is that the majority never rules. It is only the handful of economically mighty class, which decides the fate of the nation.

If political democracy is the game of numbers, then where is the majority interest of the people to rule with, to whom we can call 'we the people of India'? If it is for the people, then majority interest should reflect in policy making and its implementation. In policy makings the big industrialists and businessmen take the lion's share in their favor, despite being in minority. It only happens by virtue of their economic strength and has nothing to do with any number. If the social and economic status of the poor class is getting down day by day it is because of this fact that despite being the major portion of the society, they do not get their true and honest representation. Their elected representatives too later become merely tools in the hands of economic might and they do for them what the business houses want. The electorate feels absolutely cheated as to where go the government of the people? They should get the proper political justice and participation being the major part of 'we the people of India'. The governance through 'welfare state' means 'for the people' and not for the economically mighty ones by preference.

Women are half of the Indian population. Being such a vast majority, constitutionally they have not been conferred with any proportional political participation in democratic India. Women Reservation Bill is made to linger on in the Parliament for the reasons best known to the male dominated Indian Parliamentary system. Political justice has been 'hijacked' and that there should not be any doubt about it. There is no meaning of the concept of 'representative democracy' for the poor, middle and women class of the Indian population, if number counts by any standard in a democracy. Unless such 'majority' comes forward with a tough stand they will not be in a position to save the political democracy for them and it will remain in statute books only. The political justice will continue to be 'hijacked' by the mighty on the strength of their money. It is feared that this will not be a healthy trend for democratic India and the Constitutional visions for 'political justice' would not take much time to start collapsing with.

"If political democracy is the game of numbers,
then where is the majority interest of the people to rule with,
to whom we can call 'we the people of India'? If it is for the
people, then majority interest should reflect in policy making

and its implementation. In policy makings the big industrialists and businessmen take the lion's share in their favor, despite being in minority. It only happens by virtue of their economic strength and has nothing to do with any number."

36

Equal Protection of Laws

The concept of equal protection of laws is theoretically upright. The intention of law is also loud and clear that the law will not discriminate among people. Can the law deal with 'societal discrimination' or 'economic exploitation' to which people are perpetually subjected to from time immemorial? Without properly ensuring 'social justice' and 'economic justice' to the people, is it practically possible that the people will get "equal protection of laws" from the legal system of the country? People may argue that 'social justice' does not mean that 'equality of social status to all'. How can there be an equal social status to all? Constitutions of various countries specifically provide for State to endeavor to minimize the inequality in income among people. The Constitution expresses about serious concern with reference to disparity in income and expects the State system to remove the disparity in income. Again people may put in same question. Whether equality in income is possible? Oh... If there is no such possibility then why there is such expectation under the Constitution? Let us not play with the sentiments of the people. People may further argue that, had it been possible than the capitalistic blocks and communistic blocks would not have been there.

Historical facts reveal that various civilizations have seriously failed to ensure either 'social equality', 'economic equality' or else 'political equality' for that matter. Do we conclude that any such social protection, economic or political protection on the grounds of equality is not possible as per the historical revelations? Do we understand the concept of 'equal protection of laws' in similar references? We consider the Constitution as a 'pious book' and "we the people of India" are still waiting with a ray of hope whether how it seems to be a Justice-social, economical and political..???

The legal rights of majority of people, who are socially and economically weak, continue to be violated. The state of legal awareness is that the people even do not know as to what does a legal right mean? They do not know as to how they will get these legal rights? The person whose legal right has been violated, he himself should come and tell to the court of law. They need to hire the services of an advocate. They are poor. They are not sure whether they will get any bread for their family, by the evening. How would they be able to pay the fee of the advocates? If they are doing pairvi of the case for getting their legal rights, when they will go for work and earn bread for their kids? The kids will go without food. Either you fight 'litigations' to get your legal rights or think for earning the bread for the day. The legal rights they may get in due course provided hearing in the case is not delayed, but their kids would die of starvation that is sure. Yes…make a note of it, this is the bitter truth of the concept of 'equal protection before laws' and perhaps would be very difficult to swallow. Laws are there to provide legal aid to the needy people at the expenses of the state. Legal Services Authorities are making all out efforts in that direction. We should not at all doubt the intentions of the legal system. Making 'available' legal aid is one thing, whereas ensuring 'effective' legal aid is altogether different thing. Expert advocates have their own parameters. If the State endeavors to ensure expert and effective legal aid then to a certain extent one could say that honest steps are taken towards 'equal protection before the laws'. Let us hope for the best.

"Do we conclude that any such social protection, economic or political protection on the grounds of equality is not possible as per the historical revelations? Do we understand the

concept of 'equal protection of laws' in similar references? We consider the Constitution as a 'pious book' and "we the people of India" are still waiting with a ray of hope whether how it seems to be a Justice-social, economical and political..???"

37

Women Empowerment-A Myth

Women empowerment literally means for the women to be socially strong, for the women to be economically strong. By means of various Constitutional and statutory provisions the legal system of the country has attempted to ensure justice to the women in Indian society. The Constitutional law of India makes it expressly clear that there will be equal application of law and that there would be no discrimination on the grounds of sex. The Parliament, which is the prime legislative body, is also convinced about the sorry state of affairs of women prevalent in Indian society. That is why it comes out with legislative measures so as to ensure a better environment to the women. This concern of the Parliament is indicative of the fact that status of the women in our society is not much better and the women empowerment is not visible as expected, despite adequate legislative measures.

The foundation of women empowerment starts with basic primary education to the girl child. Now position is much better as compared to yester years. The girls have more access to primary education particularly in urban and semi-urban areas. When we come down to rural areas, no doubt things have improved due to awareness among parents towards educating girls and sending them to schools. But because of poor basic facilities in villages such schooling appears to be a myth only and is still far from reality. Better primary schooling is the back bone of strong secondary and higher education. This ultimately becomes a decisive factor towards future empowerment of women. Mere schooling is not enough for the girl children in rural areas unless there are well linked intermediate schools and degree colleges so that they can further continue with their higher studies. You go in the villages and you will find that majority of girls are either drop outs in the middle class or even if they complete their schooling successfully they are unable to further pursue their studies because of lack of higher schools facilities in the locality. If intermediate or degree colleges for the girls are there they are located far from the villages. Parents hesitate sending their girl children to such distant colleges for safety reasons. The security sense of the parents appears to be quite genuine looking to existing social scenario and rusty law and order machinery. There is a general impression not only in rural but urban areas too that the women are not safe in the society. There is no reason for any argument since such an impression weakens any initiative for women empowerment and restricts it to the extent of myth only.

Indian society now needs not only the literacy but proper education to the women which should be productive enough to generate job opportunities and satisfactory future employment to the women as per their ability and the level of merit. We have remarkable talent among our girls which remains unexplored because of certain inherent defects in our system. Proper education will socially empower the women where if she intends to go for employment, it will economically empower her. Girls seeking employment and they are in employment rubbing shoulders with male counter parts, is hardly a matter of decade. Otherwise thinking of girls going out for jobs used to be considered as social taboo. It gives an immense pleasure that women in Indian society are getting empowered, albeit on a very slow pace. Society needs to jettison its conservative approach towards women and let them provide educational infrastructure to empower with.

"You go in the villages and you will find that majority of girls are either drop outs in the middle class or even if they complete their schooling successfully they are unable to further pursue their studies because of lack of higher schools facilities in the locality. If intermediate or degree colleges for the girls are there they are located far from the villages."

38

Dilemma of Being a Girl

Why to talk about the dilemma of being a girl child? Why the society addresses the girl to be a weaker sex? By nature human existence on this earth is not possible without participation of female side. It is not the sexual side of being the weaker sex, but in fact it is the social angle of being the weaker sex. Social practices reveal that in families birth of a girl child is not that welcome as compared to birth of a boy child. If at all it happens to be a social practice than off course, it could be unarguably concluded that this practice would not have come to stay all of a sudden. It is the human mind which starts discriminating between the two sexes and it is not only discriminating but to the extent starts addressing it to be the weaker one. Have we ever examined the psychological impact of such discriminatory approaches over the girls? And the most significant dilemma to my mind is that as to whether what do we aim to achieve after all, by putting girls in the category of a weaker sex? There is no scope for any argument in agreeing to it that such discrimination makes an adverse impact on general psychology of girls and their overall future development, whether social or economical.

Let us not hesitate in accepting this biological truth that the nature itself has created the male and the female to be the opposite but equal sex. Both of them are supplementary to each other. The institution of marriage and procreation of children is impossible without the union of two sexes. Looking to this natural existence of the girl child on this earth there is no reason in addressing them to be the weaker sex. This is nothing but merely a weakness of human mind. This mind set needs to be corrected in the larger interest of social psychology and for the social protection to be given to the girl children.

Weaker sex psychology makes its dangerous impact on male-female social harmony in a manner that on one side it discourages females 'negatively' while on the other side it encourages males again 'negatively' only. The result we come across in the society in the form of crimes against women, domestic violence and most serious rape offences where the culprits do not even spare the minor girls. Gang rape incidents of girls either adults or minor are nothing but reflections of this negative encouragement by the exponents of 'weaker sex' impressions for girls. This has already proved to be a curse on the society in the sense that crimes against women are now heading towards an ugly trend. It needs to be stopped without delay. Any careless approach towards women is bound to make an adverse impact on social health. The society will become ultimately weak. The need of the hour is that we want a strong society with both the sexes intact. This is possible only when we are ready to change our mind set towards a girl child. Let this dilemma not be in the mind of a girl child that she is going to be the weaker sex in the society. Things are changing fast, no doubt, in the modern society but still there remains a lot to be done. We can do it with a positive mind set towards our girls then only our society will start thinking pragmatically and our nation will become strong. Did you ever sensibly think about it that legislative provisions for protecting women against domestic violence are very recent law enacted by Indian Parliament? Why this law for protecting our women when we claim ourselves to be an educated and modern society? Why this impression that women need to be protected from men? Can't we live together with our women as civilized society? Do we need a law to control and regulate our behavior towards women? We are yet to learn to respect our girls and the women. All is not well, there in educated India. That is the real dilemma.

"Have we ever examined the psychological impact of such discriminatory approaches over the girls? And the most significant dilemma to my mind is that as to whether what do we aim to achieve after all, by putting girls in the category of a weaker sex?"

39

Primary Education Struggles

Education is the basic requirement for well being and survival of any civilization. Primary education could be defined as the beginning of education to a child so that his foundation of thinking process by and by is made strong. Language is the mode of communication from one individual to the other. The primary education objectively inculcates the letters of the languages and imprints in the mind of the child in such a manner that slowly and slowly he develops a command over the language. It is said knowledge is power and it strengthens a person from within. Knowledge could be communicated with the help of language either through orally or in written form. If the child develops a confidence over the language he could acquire variety of knowledge from the ideas of great personalities of the world and would be able to empower himself to handle future challenges of his life. His mind becomes strong. This empowerment through knowledge would not only strengthen him individually but would also enable him to bravely face the challenges for the sake of the interest of the nation.

Let us examine the state of affairs of primary education in India. Primary education in India is in very bad shape. Not only in rural areas but in urban areas also the primary schools owned by the government are not functioning properly. Primary education in privately owned schools has been completely commercialized. It is so expensive that every middle class and people belonging to lower income groups cannot afford or even think of sending their children to these private schools. Government owned primary schools whether in urban areas or in the villages are victims of bad management. Teaching and other supporting staff in these schools is appointed on the basis of nexus between the system managers and the political managers. The meritorious aspirants for teaching assignments in these schools are completely ignored despite the fact that they are talented, hold better qualifications and other credentials. They fail to get appointment as teachers in these schools because they could not develop the 'criminal nexus' with the system managers. Bribery is the means to manage the system for procuring such appointments. They do not have the resources except for their own merit. The boys with merit could not manage money to bribe with. For such unfortunate reasons merit could not make its place in the system. When the system itself is devoid of merit you cannot expect better performance from them. The 'personnel' who have 'successfully' entered the system by corrupt means are going to further degrade it for the genuine reasons that they have no merits or morals. Resultantly such schools have gone much below the level they are expected to deliver educational justice to our small school going children. Imagine how dangerous it is going to be for our children in the primary education of these schools where they are left in unclean hands of such teaching staff? We need to re-examine the bonafide of the claims of the system with regard to delivery of educational justice. The obvious conclusion is going to be the worst and painful defeat of ends of educational justice.

Better primary education is the back bone of powerful future education of our children and strong human civilizations. We should not search for the reasons far away as to why our children are so poorly educated? Why the back bone of our primary education has been broken? The reasons are well present around us only. The children from poor families are bound to go in this government owned primary schools only. By any measure of population percentage such children are big in numbers, whether of rural or urban. Merely going schools and coming back home is of no meaning. The actual worry is that as to what all they are learning about in these schools? Those who are given with the task of delivering education are highly incapable to deliver that. What do we think then? Keep sitting with our fingers crossed. That's it. Primary education would not be able to strengthen or even survive for that matter, till the system managers keep compromising with the merit of our youth and do not come out with better capable teaching stuff following strict policy measures. We are poor because our primary education is poorly managed. We are weak because we are not properly educated. Do not blame the people of India and the poverty prevalent all around. The system managers should have the courage to come forward and own the responsibility for the damage they have already done to our primary education. It is in fact the system failure and is just not innocent one. It is the result of an intentional and well calculated 'criminal nexus' between the 'beneficiaries' of this system, while the actual sufferers, are the majority poor countrymen and their small innocent children. I am confident enough that the system managers do not have any excuse to put forward for the pathetic state of primary education in the country. They should seriously and honestly think about the primary education to the poor children. They should at least feel accountable to their inner conscience. Otherwise, we would be a country dangerously keep on balancing on the brink of survival only. Come on..!!!.. Managers, before it is too late.

"By any measure of population percentage such children are big in numbers, whether of rural or urban. Merely going schools and coming back home is of no meaning. The actual worry is that as to what all they are learning about in these schools? Those who are given with the task of delivering education are highly incapable to deliver that. What do we think then? Keep sitting with our fingers crossed. That's it."

40

Religious Secularism

This term may sound to be quite strange to many. As to what do we mean by 'religious secularism'? True... it is quite a difficult task to me as well to define 'religious secularism' with a sense of judicious balance. It goes without saying that Indian Constitution visualizes for a secular structure for the nation. But the term 'secular' was introduced in the preamble of Indian Constitution by way of 42nd Amendment only. Following "secularism" means that the state will not sponsor any religion. State will neither profess nor propagate any religion. The people in India would have a fundamental freedom of choice with regard to religious faith. India is a country where people of different religious faith reside making people to keep faith in any particular religion. Keeping faith in any particular religion cannot be enforced by law. Religion is a question of faith and belief.

What could be a religion? Off course, doing well to the people, the mankind, other living organisms and the environment. Religion could be defined as that we should have mutual respect for each other and their religious belief. We should not develop any kind of ill will against any category of people professing any religion of their choice. May be they are not practicing any religion at all but they are good people by their vision for doing well to the society and the people. Fundamental freedom of religion is also to be construed as to not to profess any religion which are existing in the modern world. It is a unique kind of religious freedom and this is the main spirit behind the prevailing concept. A person may claim that he only believes in humanity and practice humanism and that is his religion. Yes..! That is great. The 'humanism' he may introduce as giving respect to all people irrespective of their caste, creed and religion. In addition to human beings, the 'humanism' would further profess as to care and protection to all the animals and other living organisms on this earth. The protection of environment should be the prime concern to every individual for the sake of survival of the mankind, flora and fauna. Before the term secular was introduced in the preamble of the Constitution it never meant that we were not secular earlier or that we became secular only after 42nd amendment of the Indian Constitution. Being secular is a state of mind. Merely incorporating the word 'secular' in statute books would not be enough. Claiming oneself to be secular may be easier while practicing being secular is a much more difficult task. But nothing is impossible to be achieved on this earth provided we make an honest approach towards 'religious secularism' without any prejudice or any bit of vested interest or bias. Religion is to human and being human itself is a religion. Every religions existing on this earth call for mutual respect for each other. Then where the problem arises? Why then religious fanaticism all around? Why do then blood clashes with each other in the name of religion?

In one form or the other, this kind of fanaticism is being witnessed in different religious beliefs all across the world. This needs to be immediately stopped for the sake of mankind. Its human nature and even there are legal justifications that where there is an aggression the person under attack is legally entitled for his defense. An extreme aggressive situation gives an impression to the person that now attack only is the best defense. But this is no final solution. Why to arise such situation at all which gives rise to a feel of fanaticism in the mind of the people? Where such a situation has arrived at, we are sorry to say that this is flagrant breach of faith for mutual religions respect to each other. This trend is going to prove dangerous for the world peace. Religious secularism advocates for being secular religiously without interfering into other's religious beliefs. It would be possible only by practicing mutual respect to every human being by virtue of the fact that he is also a human being. No single religion could be blamed for religious fanaticism. It is the one which makes an attack first. That should be condemned without prejudice to any particular religion. That's the religious secularism.

"But nothing is impossible to be achieved on this earth provided we make an honest approach towards 'religious secularism' without any prejudice or any bit of vested interest or bias. Religion is to human and being human itself is a religion. Every religions existing on this earth call for mutual respect for each other. Then where the problem arises? Why then religious fanaticism all around? Why do then blood clashes with each other in the name of religion?"

41

A Sense of Corporate Liability

Role of corporations in our present commercial world has become very significant particularly when industrialization is at its top world around. Corporate activities are important for sound economic growth of any nation. At the same time it has a direct relationship with societal development and healthy human survival. Whenever we turn an eye towards corporate it automatically comes to our mind that it has its own profit links. Every corporate manager works with a strategy that it has to stay in the corporate world with maximum money mobilization. After commencement of the era of globalization of international commerce, corporate activities are being witnessed at a very fast pace. This is to keep in conformity with the requirements of trade and commerce, legal machineries and existing procedures are also broadly modified with a view to facilitate global trade and commerce activities among nations. The obvious and judicious motive should be to strengthen the socio-economic level and raise the standard of living of fellow human beings. Basically either there are public sector giants or private sector companies rum by big business houses Government run public sector corporations survive at the strength of investment with public money. It is noticed from last so many decades that government run public companies become victim of paralytic and mismanagement on part of the public servants clubbed with corrupt political leadership. This 'malicious nexus' is the basic factor behind reported sickness of government companies. As a result of this nexus government companies are declared 'sick' and gradually they are either wind up or sold out to private bidders at a throw away price. Very soon one can notice the difference that the same reportedly 'sick' government companies now being managed efficiently and are converted into profit earning companies for the private owner. The private owner does no magic to the company. It is only the proper strategic management of the company with a sense of belongingness for their own partisan economic gains that the 'sick' government corporate turns into a healthy business corporate.

This question always screws my mind that why there is a general complaint that the government's corporate are not managed properly and the government managers mismanage them to the core of making them 'sick'? There must be no doubt about it that the managers of the government corporate are in any way less trained or less qualified. They do know the tricks of 'business administration' to manage the business of the government to its advantage. But why the 'sickness' then, running in losses and windings up finally? Can't the government run corporate managers have a sense of belongingness for the company and for the economic strength of the nation? Can't they have the dedication and put in their all managerial skills in the interest of the nation, when they are fully qualified and completely equipped with at cost of the public money? Why the political managers and the ministers forget their representative character and start indulging in serious criminal negligence in complete disregard to the popular mandate they have been conferred by the people of India? There is nothing wrong in it when under these circumstances people are compelled to think about the 'criminal conspiracy' in rendering the government corporate to be 'sick' with a malicious motive to sell it out to some 'favorable private giant' for proportionate corresponding gain.

This question will always remain to be unanswered as to why with similar set of qualification and infrastructure the private corporate fare well? And why does government corporate fail? After the government corporate is sold to the private owner on the plea of its 'sickness' it gets good management by the same set of guiding principles of business administration and it starts functional, recovers from sickness and becomes healthy. Whom to fix the liability for this corporate failure of serious nature? Why do the corporate managers play with hard earned public money? Is for the reasons that since this money does not belong to the corporate managers that is why it should be wasted and be subjected to serious financial mismanagement and poor business administration? Human resource of such corporate is also to be blamed equally. They are absolutely negligent and careless when they are government run, but they suddenly become smart and active after the corporate is taken over by the private business house.

Is there anybody listening to it and will reply to it? Why do we not take lessons from countries like China and Japan? It is not the policy management or the guiding principles responsible for our failures but in fact it is complete lack of will power, sincerity and honesty for the sake of our nation which makes all the difference. It is no secret that the two countries have fast grown and become global corporate giants only for the reasons of their honesty, integrity, dedication and the deep sense of belongingness for their nation. Why can't we Indians? If not, then why do we not be ready to shoulder the liability for corporate failure? Let us be optimistic and must not forget that there always remains a hope provided we work.

"This question will always remain to be unanswered as to why with similar set of qualification and infrastructure the private corporate fare well? And why does government corporate fail? After the government corporate is sold to the private owner on the plea of its 'sickness' it gets good management by the same set of guiding principles of business administration and it starts functional, recovers from sickness and becomes healthy. Whom to fix the liability for this corporate failure of serious nature? Why do the corporate managers play with hard earned public money?"

42

Traditional Indian Economics

Looking to the socio-economic conditions in Indian perspectives, whether in past or as existing today we were more depending upon traditional economics like agriculture, animal husbandry, small scale cottage industries which were most suited to prevailing rural situations. Even in post-independent India things are not much better as regard the rural conditions are concerned. There is a scope for argument as to whether how long we would keep crying for traditional Indian economics particularly in an environment where the global economics is advancing very fast? Traditions are merely symbolic ones and become a matter of gone days. When the traditions do not fit into the demands and requirements of the day, then it is always preferred to make a shift from traditional approach towards much better options for fulfilling developmental needs of the day in any country. There should not be any doubt about it that developmental needs of the country today must be to keep pace with the fast moving global economics too. As claimed by our system managers on various occasions at national and international forums that we are now developing country. Meaning thereby that we are passing through a transition phase. It is a matter of common understanding that being on the way of transition is not an easy task for any country. It used to take a lot of pain through perseverance while making policy initiatives and its subsequent implementation in the same spirit, while switching over to from traditional economics to growing modern economics.

What do we mean by modern economics? I can only make my submission in layman's language as is understood commonly. Modern day economics has given rise to an environment for large scale industrialization that is an era of big machines. These machines without doubt, have enhanced production activities in a wonderful manner all across the world. The countries which have adequate industrial skills are cashing it on and have become economic force to reckon with. Why not..? Such countries have proved themselves to be economic superpowers. Putting in hard labor and thereby sharpening industrial skills cannot be monopoly of any country. Where a small country like Japan, on its own strength of honest dedicated hard labor is able to prove itself to be an economic super power in the world. For large scale industrialization the basic necessity is an uninterrupted power supply system. Although our country is in a mode for transition to modern economics and that should be always welcome. But are we in a position to honestly admit that before deciding to switch over to, we did a comprehensive home work so as to accomplish a sustainable industrial growth? I think we did not. The result is that our planning for industrial growth has been badly hampered. We could not plan to have an effective and well developed power sector which could connect the entire country. The regions which were able to successfully establish their strong power sectors unarguably they are today leading industrial regions in India, like Maharashtra, Karnataka, Gujarat, Delhi, Haryana etc. While the states like Bihar, Uttar Pradesh, Odisha, West Bengal, Madhya Pradesh are lagging far behind and the only reason being poor power sector. As on today we need to stop a bit and think over about the existing state of power infrastructure in most of our states so as to ensure a cumulative industrial growth of the nation.

The point of worry is that for the sake of transition and without prior adequate preparation at ground level, we took a decision to keep pace with modern economics without any support base to our traditional economics. Without proper power infrastructure and machines the tragedy is that the rural cottage industries are completely uprooted but as a replacement new industries could not be established. Even today one should admit honestly that in majority of the villages there is no continuous power supply. The impact of modern economics could only be witnessed in selected few regions, where they have equated with the saturation points, otherwise rest of the parts of the country are yet to witness the knocks of industrialization process. Looking to the pace of existing policy implementations and the development, it appears that it will still take years altogether which could be said to be an adequate power supply structure in all the regions of the country. But there appears to be no immediate alternative proposals from the managers of small scale and cottage industrial sectors to protect the traditional Indian economics and save it from complete collapse.

"The point of worry is that for the sake of transition and without prior adequate preparation at ground level, we took a decision to keep pace with modern economics without any support base to our traditional economics. Without proper power infrastructure and machines the tragedy is that the rural cottage industries are completely uprooted but as a replacement new industries could not be established."

43

Unity in Diversity

Unity in diversity is said to be very relevant with reference to India. In India there are various kinds of differential situations. Like regional differentials, linguistic differentials, differentials on caste and religious lines. We keep nature born gender differentials in the same category. It is not an easy task to talk about 'unity in diversity'. It also becomes very difficult to say whether diversity, differentiality are synonymous terms. The very simple meaning of unity in diversity appears to be that we are diverse whether in the name of language, in the name of region, caste or religion, but still we are one. We have no differences in the name of diversities. We do not fight with each other, we do respect the feelings of diversity among us that's why we talk about unity in diversity. We should feel proud of it. We do feel pride yes..! So we never tire of talking about unity in diversity. At least we lose nothing in talking about all that. In fact it is very simple to keep talking the things. Good talks sound good at least. Bad things should not be told, otherwise they go 'naked' and would not look good. The innocent people of India are made to be in the habit of, to keep listening to good things. How could the people keep talking good things be made guilty of it when such talks do not happen the way they talk them to be? This would be a matter of serious concern.

Jurist Roscoe Pound put emphasis for making of laws for the reasons of 'conflict of individual interests' in the society. He was of the firm opinion that due to existence of differential situations in the society people develop 'vested interest' in them. If there appears to be any hurdle in fulfillment of their vested interests then talking about things like 'unity' is of no meaning. Individual interests come in conflict with. Then laws are broken, maintenance of law and order is breached. We come across reported instances of loss of life and property belonging to the people. Talking about 'social unity' under the shadow of 'social justice' appears merely to be a bookish talk.

Society in India has been a very painful history in the name of unity on caste lines and in the name of religions. Majority of castes in India could never be united. Though we claim ourselves to be a secular country but frankly speaking number of religions could never be put on a single platform. Well planned situations of 'bloodshed' are made to happen. On the basis of 'regional feelings' and 'language' we never find ourselves united. The system of reservation in public employment was made 'caste based' instead of 'class based'. The argument was that there was such an intermixing of different 'classes' with the 'castes' that it appeared to be very difficult to separate them. Looking it from castiest angle it becomes compulsion of the system for the reasons of deep rooted caste system in Indian society. In the event of projected 'conflict of interest' then definitely there are going to be polarized groups of 'pro-reservationists' as well as 'anti-reservationists'. Now would you be able to talk about unity? Possibly not. Serious conflict of mutual vested interests between the two groups would be clearly visible. This conflict would give rise to law and order problem in the society and the law would not be in a position to stop it. We should keep it in our mind that caste based diverse mentality has also its deep roots within the law and order administration system as well. What you could do then after all? Whether it is executive or judiciary they are also parts of this social system only and are also under the pressures of multiple social obligations.

Do we need to talk about unity in religious diversity? Talking about demolishing 'mosques' and constructing 'temples' are the facets of 'unity in diversity' we relish? We would have to see through within ourselves and then think upon as to what extent we are 'united one'? Whenever in our society there is an occasion of any religious or social festivity of different communities, we witness heavy deployment of paramilitary forces by the administration at every nook and corner of the cities. What does it indicate? Administration is aware that the 'local police' would prove to be a failure in maintaining religious and social solidarity even at the gun point? There is a religious diversity and it should be welcomed in the sense that there is a freedom of choice of religion to everyone. But where has gone the unity? The administration takes a sigh of relief after a prolonged tense situation. Hey Almighty …. All went well after all, there was no bloodshed among the religiously diverse communities, everything went off 'peacefully'.

Linguistic diversity is bit problematic. Possibly India would be the only country in the entire world where various provinces are constituted on the basis of linguistic diversity only. Its mere completion of formality only to say that language Hindi would be the language of the nation. That's all. Otherwise there is no need to say that on number of occasions Hindi language had to be dishonored at the hands of regional languages. It is well if it is limited to the extents of disrespect only. If it appears to people that somehow attempts are being made to impose Hindi then without much delay linguistic unity is thrashed to pieces in the entire nation. Law and order problem could be witnessed all around.

Whenever, we come across people talking that one is 'north Indian' the other one is 'south Indian' at that moment itself regional unity is fragmented. What is the harm if we all claim to be Indian only? Article 19 of the Indian Constitution confers fundamental freedom to its citizens to settle down in any region or part of the country, but the moment fanatic regionalism of political leaders speaks high then there is no need to say that this issue is made so sensitive that people of other regions are beaten to run away from that region. They leave saying that they are getting back to their 'native places' as if India is not their native place and they have gone to settle at any outside place within India. Serious consequences would follow in the form of enmity of untold nature. Executive and Judiciary look to be absolutely helpless and the 'unity in diversity' are heading towards complete fragmentation. We need to take honest concrete efforts to stop it before it goes too late.

"Society in India has been a very painful history in the name of unity on caste lines and in the name of religions. Majority of castes in India could never be united. Though we claim ourselves

to be a secular country but frankly speaking number of religions could never be put on a single platform. Well planned situations of 'bloodshed' are made to happen. On the basis of 'regional feelings' and 'language' we never find ourselves united."

———————————————

44

Living with Human Dignity

Defining human dignity is a very complicated task. Every person takes birth as a human. There are number of social situations which compel individuals to pass their life even worse than animals. Human dignity could be merely statements written in books or clamoring made during speeches and conferences. But when the things are seen at the ground levels of practicality, then off course, the reality is worth not to be stated. Whenever we would talk about 'human dignity' we will talk about 'humanity'. Talking about living ones in the nature then mainly there are humans, animals or insects. Human beings have acquired a better status then animals for the reasons that they could better use their mind. Development of human mind, his imagination power and tendency to enforce upon the imaginations separates them from animal existence.

In world Constitutions a very basic right for human existence has been mentioned and that is 'right to life'. Right to life includes the 'right to live with human dignity'. Other numbers of basic rights are also provided which are visualized at international levels in the form of 'universal declaration of human rights'. Visualizations are good, which should be the natural result of our honest perceptions towards life thoughts, in which our genuine concerns must reflect. Particularly in the sense that our such visualizations should not merely remain into documents only but they should be worked upon in a manner that such rights make a strong grip even to the last human being on this earth. These all basic rights and their enjoyment should not be restricted merely to a handful of persons. Its need not to say, but this only is the bitter truth. In reality these rights in the society are in fact available to handful of people only. For maximum percentage of population, the people are compelled to live even in worse inhuman conditions. What to talk about their living with human dignity? Let us see that if they were not able to live with human dignity than at least they should get a human death. Unfortunately that is also not in their destiny. Throughout their life they and their kids struggled for food so that they can fill up their stomach and one day all of sudden they starved to death. Lifelong they suffered from malnutrition. There was no strength left in their body. People threw their dead body away in the nearby river. There was no much water left in the river. The dead body remained lying there decomposing, stinking. It was eaten away by crows, vultures and rowdy dogs. This way the humanity came to an end. It was a hopeless and relentless search by that man to live with human dignity. But he could not. People feel relieved, that's good at least the earth became free from the burden of that man. Such people are in fact burden only in the eyes of today's materialistic world, isn't it? The human being was dead but the humanity could not muster him the human feel even. Here people sell out the 'qafan' of dead bodies also.

So to live with human dignity has been covered under Article 21 of right to life. Meaning thereby, right to live with human dignity is a fundamental right. In a country like India official data are testimony to the fact that of overall population, about thirty percent people of it live below the poverty line. Almost similar percentage of the population is either on the poverty line or around it. We should be ready to accept the bitter truth that about sixty to seventy percent of India's population is struggling with poverty situations. They do not know in the morning whether they will get the bread in the evening or not. Even if they get the bread, it is not sufficient enough to mitigate the hunger of the kids and the family. They may get one piece of bread to eat and rest of the stomach they fill up with water. There is no shelter for them, no proper clothes on the body. Animals live naked like that. No please… humans too live naked.

However, in our Constitution there is a visualization of welfare state. Now to what extent we are able to do welfare of the people, this needs to be seen? A nation will be made, where there is social equality and no economic inequality. It will be the liability of the state that for people's welfare and progress, state should ensure such a social system which at least could reflect in an effective manner the social justice and economic justice in national life of the country. Let us leave behind political justice. First the people should get the bread with peace. You are free to blame me that it is all negative. Why the positive side of the national system is being overlooked? I will be given a lesson that in the event where a glass is half filled with water and half empty then being positive, I should look for the glass half filled. No… please! I need a reply from the administration of the system that even after sixty seven years of independence, why the glass is half empty till now? This glass 'half empty' is in fact sixty to seventy percent of our population which throughout its life struggles in poverty and ultimately dies in poverty. The glass is left half empty and it continues to be half empty for decades and decades and I am being given lessons to think positive, talk positive and do not look to the half empty side of the glass. No…sorry. It has now become my habit to keep looking the half empty side of the glass and keep questioning the national system about it. Yes… I will see the negativity. Humanity is clamoring for justice of dignity. When the people will get rid of poverty and become economically prosperous? Is there anybody listening to it..? I am hopeful to see the people getting out of poverty conditions and live with human dignity.

"Throughout their life they and their kids struggled for food so that they can fill up their stomach and one day all of sudden they starved to death. Lifelong they suffered from malnutrition. There was no strength left in their body. People threw their dead body away in the nearby river. There was no much water left in the river. The dead body remained lying there decomposing, stinking. It was eaten away by crows, vultures and rowdy dogs. This way the humanity came to an end. It was a hopeless and relentless search by that man to live with human dignity. But he could not. People feel relieved, that's good at least the earth became free from the burden of that man. Such people are in fact burden only in the eyes of today's materialistic world, isn't it? The human being was dead but the humanity could not muster him the human feel even. Here people sell out the 'qafan' of dead bodies also."

45

Offences Against Women Unabated

Under any period of civilization, women remain to be half of the population. But whatever the civilization it may be, in every era it was dominated by male patriarchal psychology. As a matter of fact the women being human are to be kept at par with men as per the statutory institutions of the world. But the pertinent question is that whether in the present time the women are able to get their equal status in the society in true sense as intended by law? Let us not talk about law. There are lot many things written in law. We talk about gender justice that there would be no discrimination on the grounds of sex. We take a kind of pledge about it. But finally what happens? There we come across increasing trends of crimes against women in the society. Are we able to give that respect to the women? The respect they deserve by virtue of the fact they being better half of the male population. No..! Certainly not.

If we talk about sexual offences only then rape is the worst offence in the life of any women. If offences take place against women that too the like of hateful offence of this kind, then the question arises that who is guilty after all for the cruel offence of rape? The humanity goes 'dead' when we come across the cases where minor girls are made victims of rape by this so-called civilized society. You would be thinking that in fact to whom we wish to hold guilty? No..! No..! I leave it up to you to make a judgment about it, under the circumstances where our innocent girls are not safe. How to make our girls believe that we are not uncivilized? That there is no need for them to worry about. We are out there to see them back home safe. This should not be a matter of worry or of feeling concerned for the women but it should be a matter of serious introspection for the people who claim them to be a civilized one, well educated and living in an advanced society.

This only is the society where women had no right to live and they used to be killed in the name of tradition of committing sati, whose husband was dead. The cruel tradition had been that the widow woman had to die 'live' on the death pyre of her husband. Today also the widow women are seen with a very hateful eye by the so-called advanced society. On ceremonial occasions their presence is considered to be unwelcome. Okay take for instance laws have been made. Tradition of sati has been prohibited and defined as an offence. Widows are also given right to 'live'. Those abetting a widow to commit sati would be punished. But how to mould thinking of the people in society? Society would leave such widows in complete isolation up to their fate to die ultimately. How to infuse a sense of 'social acceptability' for such widow women? Law appears to be absolutely helpless.

Dowry tortures and consequent deaths are not the matters of gone days. Today's modern world, which is knocking to settle on the moon, the married women are badly humiliated for the offence they never did. Their offence is that they did not bring dowry with them at the time of marriage. Their offence is that they took birth in a poor family which failed to arrange dowry for them. We do not even bother to burn them alive and kill. Law of the country keeps taking its course only afterwards. Feticides are the 'achievements' of the advances made in the fields of science and technology by this ultra-modern society. Female feticide has increased in such large numbers that this offence has started dangerously affecting the 'sex-ratio' in the society. If girl's population will be continuously made to reduce in this fashion and the natural balance of sex-ratio is made to be disturbed then without doubt sexual offences against girls would increase dangerously. Feticide has been declared to be crime but still unstoppable. What the laws could do if the people in the society are out to break their own laws? Doing crimes to the extent to commit rape with their own girls and kill them ruthlessly in the mother's womb itself. Oh..! Almighty help us out. These unabated offensive trends against women would destroy the social fabric completely.

If we wish to reduce offences against women, then as a civilized society, we would have to change our mindset towards the women. We would have to take a pledge to honor the women. Ensure initiatives in the definitive sense so that they get their rights. It is for us to see that women should not be treated as commodities to be enjoyed by men. Otherwise our coming generations would never excuse us. Do not forget that a society which fails to learn to respect its women is cursed to be doomed by divine forces. To see that the legal system of any country works, unless the people of that country extend their honest, active and unblemished co-operation, we would not be in a position to stop offences against women in the society. Now it is for us to see that laws of the nation work in a proper and effective manner. There would be no need of laws to regulate us provided we learn to behave ourselves. Let us come forward to establish the respect for the women. This only would be the great justice free from any gender bias. For this purpose we do not need a court system but we need a just and fair social system.

"If we wish to reduce offences against women, then as a civilized society, we would have to change our mindset towards the women. We would have to take a pledge to honor the women. Ensure initiatives in the definitive sense so that they get their rights. It is for us to see that women should not be treated as commodities to be enjoyed by men. Otherwise our coming generations would never excuse us. Do not forget that a society which fails to learn to respect its women is cursed to be doomed by divine forces."

46

Merely Making Laws is not Enough

There is a very critical saying which teases my mind on occasions that India is known for maximum of legislations but minimum of implementations. This general impression is really insulting to the legislature as a Constitutional body. How does one feel? That the rules he made are not implemented. Honestly speaking not in good taste. It goes without saying that Constitution provides for 'separation of powers' among three bodies, the Legislature, the Executive and the Judiciary. The legislature has to perform the function of law making, which it does. Merely making laws is not enough, provided it is not properly implemented by the executive. Laws are made to control and regulate social evils as per the popular demand. Off course, popular demand means 'We the people of India'. It has the 'force' of it. This popular force virtually goes useless when it is seen that social evils still persist and the law remains inside the statute books only. What the use of making such laws, when we are not able to apply such laws preventing the social wrongs or crimes? For the sake of implementation it is so careless and ineffective that virtually it makes no impact on the wrong doers.

The situation is quite gruesome. One may understand helplessness of the system when there is no law to handle the social wrong. The carelessness of the system goes beyond any limits of understanding when it is noticed that the laws are very much there to deal with an offence in the society, but the system absolutely fails to implement it and the crimes go unabated. Oh no..! Do not look for lame excuses. This is seriously criminal. You are a full-fledged system. Completely equipped with legal force of the nation. Still looking for petty excuses for your lack of will and faulty decision making to effectively implement the laws. For your lack of proper action and the bad governance the ultimate sufferer are the people, who are innocent ones and feel pity about you- the system. It sounds quite strange but true that our legislature has no control over the executive to ensure effective implementation of legislation so made by the competent legislative bodies under the Constitutional law. So once law is made, now it is for the executive to enforce it. Who is there to fix accountability for non-implementation of the statutes? Is it not the concern of law makers to see that why laws are not being implemented? Every legislation has its own aims and objectives to achieve with. Effective implementation of the laws is the only means by which the system could claim that the law has successfully achieved its objectives. But when we are going by saying of 'minimum implementation' then off course, it is going to be safely concluded that in the event of lack of proper implementation the very objective behind legislation stands defeated.

A simple example of dowry prohibition law would be sufficient in favor of aforesaid saying. Quite true. It is visible also. Despite the fact that there are stringent legal provisions made by the Parliament to deal with social offence of dowry but because of its poor implementation the law has absolutely failed to have its impact. Dowry related cases like tortures and bride burnings are regularly reported taking place in the society. There could be long list of such legislations which are failures because of poor implementation. This is a very sad part of Indian legislative system. There needs to be a strict constitutional provision to establish a kind of co-ordination between the makers of law and the executors of law, otherwise there is a reasonable apprehension of failure of legal machinery in the system. It would not be fair on part of justice administration. If there are legislations to prevent any social crime and still crime takes place because of poor implementation, meaning thereby that there is no rule of law. Then how to help out the system that is a big question? We should not forget that 'parliamentary democracy' envisages the accountability of the council of ministers to the legislature, the elected representatives of 'We the people of India'.

"Is it not the concern of law makers to see that why laws are not being implemented? Every legislation has its own aims and objectives to achieve with. Effective implementation of the laws is the only means by which the system could claim that the law has successfully achieved its objectives."

47

You Have a Role to Play

In whatever role an individual is in the society. If every such individual does justice to his role. Where is the scope for any kind of injustice in the society? Even if a person has a normal level of thinking ability, still he has the capacity to distinguish between as to what is fair or what is unfair, under given situations? Mind of every rational individual is very judicious. It takes its all decisions accordingly. In logical support of its decisions the mind has its own effective arguments as well. On the grounds of its force of arguments and on the strength of its will power it makes its strong footing. Every individual has the mental capacity to do it, provided his mind does not give any room for malicious feelings. The moment malicious feelings enter into the mind of an individual they capture the entire mental faculty and prevent the mind to think upon logically. The mind gets adversely affected by such negative malice and goes bias. Malicious feeling is a negative thinking which is born in the background of dishonest intention of a man. If you happen to minutely examine the behavioral side of human mind, you will clearly find that fixed centre points of positive impulse and negative impulses are already present in the human mind.

It is mostly seen that in comparison to positive ones negative impulses are much stronger. Once the negative impulses engulf over the positive ones then it is very tough for a person to get rid of it. When overpowered the negative side dominantly reflects in human behaviors. The entries of negative impulses in the human mind instigate him to commit injudicious and unfair behaviors. Whereas, positive impulses in a person generate strong will power to act in an unbiased, fair and judicious manner. It may sound to be quite unnatural but it is true that negative thinking of a man give him a strange kind of sadistic pleasure. Under the influence of such impulses the man does not care of justice or injustice. Whatever he does then or decides to do go wrong and unjust. You may notice that it is only the impact of all around negative thinking within the society that all is not well therein. Laws are broken ruthlessly, crimes are committed mercilessly. Society indulges in what amounts to be injustice. The result is that ultimately the society gets weaker and weaker.

The judiciary is the last hope for an individual in the society where he has a full confidence that he will get justice. The judiciary has no magic stick with it. It has to perform the task of delivering justice by following legal procedure. Our judges are considered to be the figures of positive impulses. They are, in an utmost unbiased manner, able to give judgments and punishing the wrongdoer by conducting hearing through trial proceedings in criminal matters or settle the disputes of civil nature. It is possible only due to their strong willpower generating out of their deep positive impulses. My humble submission is that if the people too in our society infuse positive thinking in their mindset then any of their acts or decisions would not go wrongful. Then where is the question of any injustice? The people in society would behave justly and fairly.

We should not think in a manner that we cannot have any role in the probity of our individual and social behaviors. Every individual has a feeling of probity in his mind. But under the societal situations of conflict of their vested interests he develops a kind of weakness. Knowing it fully well that his vested interest is not justified, but still he could not distance him from it and commits the wrong. Only the forces of negative impulses inside him make him to act in an unlawful manner so as to justify his stand. Ultimately he does injustice and then judiciary has to step in. If people in our society do strengthen the probity side of their mindset intact then possibly laws would not be broken and there would be no reason for injustice against any individual.

In fact the question remains whether is this all possible? Leave aside the talk of vested interests which could be justified to a certain extent. There are number of such circumstances we come across created by the people with dishonest interest. They go on fearlessly usurping over the rights of other people and forcibly dispossess them from their due rights. This is the extreme side of negative impulse. Better not to talk about probity. If the person dispossessed is capable enough to settle the scores by muscle power he does it by taking it all straight to the streets. Those not capable enough would take recourse to the legal system of the country and wait for the judicial verdict. The judiciary would not be able to help them once they are out on the street.

You must be thinking that whatever I have submitted above is all practically possible? Yes..! What you thinking is right. I too do agree with you. It is difficult in fact but it is not impossible. Possibly we dream to establish 'Ramrajya' in India. The very foundation of it is purported to be over the aforementioned possibilities only. There is a proverb 'live and let live'. See..! Every that thing is possible which comes within the limits of human domain. What is needed is that an honest and meaningful initiatives in a rightful direction. Let that initiative be individual. It shall make the room and call for a collective initiative very soon. Every individual has an urge for probity. Our role for the sake of probity is very strong provided we are determined. There happens to be a time that journey to the moon was impossible. Today human being has reached on the moon. We made it possible. Yes..! It is possible. We need to understand our role in terms of probity and do justice to our fellow beings. Yes..! Come on!!!

"Malicious feeling is a negative thinking which is born in the background of dishonest intention of a man. If you happen to minutely examine the behavioral side of human mind, you will clearly find that fixed centre points of positive impulse and negative impulses are already present in the human mind."

48

Self-Employment & Opportunities

It may be true that the State would not be in a position to provide government employment to each and every citizen. One may argue that unemployment among youth is a global phenomenon. There are reported statistics that for the reasons of unemployment the youth are unable to meet out their day to day necessary expenses. This is resulting in generating property and other related crimes in the society. We cannot blame our youth for it. To protect our youth from mental state of frustration, we need to have an honest employment policy in the country. This should not only generate employment in the public sector and in the government but at the same time it should create such an environment through its fiscal policies, socio-economic initiatives at District, Blocks and Panchayat levels that could provide self-employment opportunities for the youth. Development based project formulations are very helpful in creating a kind of environment in which our youth could themselves search for their self-employment. Our youth want to work provided they have employment. We should not forget that our youth travel from one part of the country to the other in search of employment. It is only when they fail to get work that they are attracted towards crimes. Why to blame them if we fail to provide them work environment?

Because of large scale corruption in public life, even if one claims that self-employment opportunities are generated but they have proved to be disastrous and the problem of unemployment is increasing day by day. The framers of the employment policies blame it to the increasing rate of population in the country which happens to be directly proportional to the increasing rate of unemployment according to their calculations.

We will not be in a position to generate self-employment opportunities unless as a nation we become socio-economically strong. Socio-economic strength of the nation has been badly hampered by the 'white collar criminals'. White collar criminals are worst than unemployed youth criminals. One indulges in crimes out of economic needs while the other has lust for the money to become white collar criminal. Blame game is to just divert the attention from the point in issue. Our legal machinery has been completely failed to contain this nature of criminality. Since our socio-economic fabric has been thrashed by such white collar criminals, the result is the growing unemployment among youth.

We need to give a relook to our policy relating to free market economy. It has completely ruined our indigenous economic structure. Small scale and cottage industries in the villages used to provide sufficient self-employment opportunities to our rural youth. Now after the commencement of free markets the cottage industries are completely destroyed and rural youth are moving towards urban areas in search of employment. At least rural youth should not be blamed for growing urbanization? Where should they go then? Providing employment and providing employment opportunities are two distinct areas. Where are the opportunities for employment? Who is to prepare the environment for employment generation? I have my own doubts in my mind whether multinational companies would be of any help in affording opportunities for self-employment to our youth? If the State fails so fail the youth. The State has adequate resources for generating employment but lesser political will to work upon it.

"We need to give a relook to our policy relating to free market economy. It has completely ruined our indigenous economic structure. Small scale and cottage industries in the villages used to provide sufficient self-employment opportunities to our rural youth."

49

Economic Justice-Internationally

What do we mean by economic justice? That too, within the framework of international standards. Barring a few rich countries like U.S.A., Russia, France, Britain, Germany, Japan, China, and Korea and Arab countries for that matter, the overall situation of many poor countries in the world is far from satisfactory. Economics has a direct and proportional relationship with the bare survival of human beings on this earth. It's as simple as that. If they have money they are able to get food for themselves and for the kids and would be able to survive. Its bare survival only. Do not talk about the quality food. Malnutrition and millions going without food is not uncommon in the modern international society.

Let it be any international parameter whatsoever, economic justice anywhere in the world would always mean 'no economic disparity' in the socio-economic system. What could be the international parameter to minimize the gap between people who are extremely rich and the people who are living in acute poverty conditions? Whatever the New International Economic Orders (N.I.E.O.) we are witnessing, it is preferably for generating an international environment for favorable trade and development conditions. My humble submission is that it should not be misunderstood as a mere criticism, nor that my approach is in a sense negative.

My humble question is that who is going to be the beneficiary of N.I.E.O.? Whether the 'big majority' or a 'simple minority'? Do I need to explain as to 'big majority'? Whether the N.I.E.O. has been successful in reducing the wide gap of economic disparity all across the globe? Where is the global 'inclusive growth'? Whether the system is capable to ensure that the calculated benefits of international economic order percolates downright up to the bottom? Let us not hesitate in accepting the bitter truth that the benefits of the 'new order' are monopolized within the hands of mighty few economic giants. Forget about the people who are hopelessly at down bottom. Is this economic justice? Starvation deaths are the order of the day, because the people have no money to feed them. This is a simple economics. Let the N.I.E.O. feel and ensure to the basic minimum necessities of the world poor for the sake of saving the mankind. Economic prosperity of nations is always welcome. There could be a strong argument in favor that they worked hard so they are economically prosperous. That's true. What a poor needs is the support so that he can survive then work hard and then sustain. Work is to human. But looking to the trends internationally reducing economic disparity is still a day dream.

My humble question is that who is going to be the beneficiary of N.I.E.O.? Whether the 'big majority' or a 'simple minority'? Do I need to explain as to 'big majority'? Whether the N.I.E.O. has been successful in reducing the wide gap of economic disparity all across the globe? Where is the global 'inclusive growth'? Whether the system is capable to ensure that the calculated benefits of international economic order percolates downright up to the bottom?

50

Domestic Violence-A Curse

It is a very painful situation for the Indian society or any society for that matter there are instance of domestic violence against women. It becomes more shameful when the society while claiming to be well educated, modern and civilized never hesitates to be violent. Domestic violence is a curse on the society. It has not only made its serious impact on Indian soil but it is being practiced in equally serious proportions in other parts of the world as well. Looking from the angles of legal dimensions in domestic violence women are exploited socially, economically, physically, emotionally and sexually at the hands of her husband or his relatives. Domestic violence is less a legal problem but is more a social problem. In the sense it is the polluted mindset of the people in male dominated society which needs to be overhauled otherwise the legislation will prove to be a futile exercise. Law would not be in a position to help the women victim of domestic violence while the families would keep breaking.

The burning question of the day is that do we really need a law to protect our women from domestic violence? Should we not agree that we only put the women to domestic violence? Can't we self-discipline ourselves? Do we live with this impression that only the law of the land will regulate our behavior towards the women? We are only scared of law and not of our inner conscience?

Feel within yourself. Is it not blameworthy? Legislations for protection of women from domestic violence are indications to this very fact that the women in our society are not safe even within their domestic premises. The Parliament of India is convinced about it and had to come forward with law to provide women the needed protection from domestic violence. If the women are not safe within the four walls of their home itself, then let us forget about their safety when they are out in the society at large.

What is the remedy available to the women who are victims of domestic violence? In any case the women would have to make a complaint against her husband, her in-laws or the relatives of the husband before the appropriate authority as provided under the law. Such a situation will never be tolerated and welcome by the family members. Here comes the real trouble for the women. How long the law will be in a position to provide 'protection' to the women? There are women who remain tight lipped against the incidents of domestic violence just for the sake of their kids and family interests. They keep bearing all the violence because they know that they would be the final losers. Law is not in a position to do justice to the women, despite of the fact that we have a complete law to protect the women from domestic violence. It would remain in statute books only. Let us do justice with them and the society should shun domestic violence against the women. Let us not forget that the women are an integral part of the domestic relationships. The relationship needs to be strengthened in the larger interest of the family and the society as well. Otherwise families will be broken and shattered. Repenting on afterwards, should not be the destiny of the mankind. We are here to make our own and the destiny of the nation by respecting women for a stronger society.

"The burning question of the day is that do we really need a law to protect our women from domestic violence? Should we not agree that we only put the women to domestic violence? Can't we self-discipline ourselves? Do we live with this impression that only the law of the land will regulate our behavior towards the women? We are only scared of law and not of our inner conscience? Feel within yourself. Is it not blameworthy?"

51

Compensatory Justice-Rape?

Compensation to the victims of crime is a concept which shows the helplessness of the criminal justice system. Compensation is awarded to the victims of crime when the system realizes that under the circumstances it has failed to do any justice to the person in true sense so, he be compensated for all that. Compensatory justice categorically denotes the failure of criminal justice system since it has failed to prevent crimes in the society. Crimes keep happening and keep awarding compensation. That's it. Police being one of the four pillars of the system has been conferred with statutory duty of prevention of crime in the society. When there is a breach of duty on part of the police and they fail to prevent and control crimes in the society, the ultimate sufferers are innocent victims of the crime. The system helplessly goes for compensation since it finds it difficult to enforce the duty on part of the law enforcement agencies.

Rape is the most heinous crime in the life of women. They are the victims of rape by virtue of the fact that they are the poor opposite sex in the eyes of the male dominated social psychology. They are considered to be commodities to be enjoyed rather than an individual entity as a human being and better half of the society. Why do rape are committed in the society? Do we have no respect for dignity of the women? Where the rape has been committed on women, the law comes into motion after the First Information Report (FIR) has been registered. It is very difficult to get eye witnesses in the offence of rape. By convicting the rapist and punishing him under the law, it is considered that justice is done to the woman, the victim of rape.

Merely awarding punishment to the rapist does not mean that justice has been done to the women. It is going to be a lifelong trauma and mental agony for the women who have been raped. She is in fact getting punishment for the failure of law enforcement agencies. This is absolute injustice to the woman. Now who will marry the woman who is a rape victim? Is there any law on this earth which can restore the dignity of the women so raped? No..! Now the dignity and self-respect of the woman cannot be restored. The justice system is also convinced and helpless to do any justice to the woman. The apex court comes forward with the concept of 'compensatory justice'. Let the women raped be compensated. Utter helplessness of the apex court of the country. The system appears to be not in a position to guarantee that the women in society will not be raped and will be protected. If they are victims of rape compensation will be a guaranteed. The burning question to the administrators of criminal justice is that whether we are pricing the honor of the women? Whether we are compensating the dignity of the women? Why are we so weak and helpless after all? The women are paying price for being women and getting victims of rape. Who will ensure them the safety they need? The system only. Who else? System is ready to pay compensation for rape but does not appear to make any categorical declaration that henceforth, there will be no offence of rape in the society. The better half of the society demands justice and not the compensation. Justice should not only be done but it should appear to have been done. Let us respect the dignity of the women. Compensating the raped women is not the way out. Rapes must be stopped in the society. That is the only way to ensure justice to the dignity of the women and protecting their honor.

"The burning question to the administrators of criminal justice is that whether we are pricing the honor of the women? Whether we are compensating the dignity of the women? Why are we so weak and helpless after all? The women are paying price for being women and getting victims of rape. Who will ensure them the safety they need? The system only. Who else?"

52

Educational Justice- the Mafias

Proper education has been the backbone of human civilizations. It has been directly linked with the overall societal development and advancement of a nation. If you wish to see a nation to be a weak nation, spoil its educational resources. The nation is gone. Investment in the fields of 'quality education' should be the primary agenda of any country. In India we have an education policy but the prevailing education policy is not adequate in promoting the educational justice. Educational justice means education to all irrespective of their sex, caste, religion, region or economic status. There should be equality of opportunity to all to get quality education. We watch that even after sixty seven years of independence, we in India are still struggling for education to all. Introducing Article 21-A to the Constitution of India, only in the year 2002, for Right to Education is an evidence to this effect. We often come across sex discrimination in individual families where they prefer that the boys in the family only go for better education. Whereas, the girls in the family are not given similar preference in favor of their quality education. This is due to male dominated patriarchal mentality of the society. Caste considerations are also found to be socially prevalent though the legal system of the country prohibits such considerations based upon caste or sex.

With the passage of time in the so-called modern society, we appear more inclined towards commercialization of the education system. No doubt with this commercialization, we feel that there would be an improvement in the quality of education. But the tragedy of the system is that the advantage of this 'quality education' is available to the children of those families only who could sustain it economically. All of sudden we watch an upsurge of education mafias who are out to sell education for money. They provide the 'students' every facility on 'contract' right from writing of the examination to the declaration of results with top ranks. This is not possible without the 'collusion' with the officials of education department. It is all in the knowledge of the governments but they have shut their eyes to the encouragement of such education mafias.

In the present era the government schools are struggling for their survival and are pushed on the verge of collapse. Similar is the situation in the fields of higher education. It is all public sector educational institutions Vs private sector educational institution. By introducing fundamental right to education the Constitution of India makes provisions for 25% reservation in the private sector school, in favor of the children belonging to poor and weaker sections of the society. The expenses incurred for educating such children would be borne by government exchequer. Merely introducing such provisions is not enough. The private schools are not admitting such children on one pretext or the other. The government machinery has failed to enforce this provision in its true letters and spirit. The children from poor families and weaker sections are not able to get good quality education for lack of money. Such children are majority in number. The governments are completely indifferent about it. With this poor educational backbone of majority of our children, we can easily expect as to what would be the future strength of our nation? We will continue to be weak unless we make our education strong.

"Educational justice means education to all irrespective of their sex, caste, religion, region or economic status. There should be equality of opportunity to all to get quality education. We watch that even after sixty seven years of independence, we in India are still struggling for education to all. Introducing Article 21-A to the Constitution of India, only in the year 2002, for Right to Education is an evidence to this effect."

53

Consumer Justice

Consumer justice is a very sensitive concept. A consumer is a person who consumes 'goods' or avails 'services' for a price. A consumer has no commercial gain out of such purchase of goods. He purchases those goods for his own personal domestic use. Purchasing goods for a price or availing services for a price come within the ambit of consumer laws. If there are 'defect in goods' or 'deficiency in services' it would amount to be cheating for the consumer. Thus arise a consumer dispute. The consumer spends his hard earned money for purchasing goods but would not be able to enjoy it for the defects in the goods. He spends money for availing services but finds deficiency in such services despite the payment of the price. This is grave injustice. The consumer laws are in the category of welfare legislations. The approach of justice would be inclined in favor of the consumer so as to ensure the welfare of the consumer for the price he spent. The 'consumerism' starts with conferring various statutory rights to the consumers of the goods and the services and which are to be protected by legal system of the country.

The concept of consumer justice came as an exception to the rule of *'caveat emptor'*. Rule of *caveat emptor* literally means 'buyer be aware'. That is why we see display boards on consumer stores that 'goods once sold shall not be returned'. This rule puts a burden on the buyer that before purchasing any goods from the market the buyer should first satisfy himself about the quality and utility of the goods up to his requirements and then purchase the goods. Later on if the buyer finds that the goods are not up to his requirements and wants to return the goods, the seller has every right to refuse to accept the goods. This rule would be applicable provided at the time of purchasing the goods the buyer had an opportunity to himself physically inspect the goods.

One may fail to understand whether it is the burden of the buyer only to testify about the quality of goods? Where the buyer has the skill to check the quality of the goods at the time of purchase? Why the rule of *caveat emptor* does not impose any liability on the seller to sell quality goods? Why this risk to the buyers only? This is altogether a different thing that in the era of consumerism, the rule of 'let the buyer be aware' is not applicable in case of consumer purchases. But still this rule is open to misuse. Arguments are that this rule continues to be in the statute books for 'commercial purchases' only. But this would in no way be justified where the burden is on the side of the buyer only. In the markets full of below quality goods, how the buyer would be in a position to pick up the quality goods? For no fault of the buyer relating to maintaining the quality of goods, he would have to ultimately suffer at the hands of legal system. The rule needs to be suitably amended so as to judiciously balance between rights of a buyer vis-à-vis duties of a seller.

It is very sad when society comes across abundance of adulterated food being sold freely in markets. It is well within the knowledge of the administrators of the system also. Who cares? It is dangerously criminal. It not only causes serious health hazards to the consumers in the society but it costs the life of the consumers too. The matters relating to sale of adulterated food or even making or storing of such adulterated food for purpose of selling it to the consumers are to be dealt with under the rule of 'strict liability'. This rule makes mere possession of adulterated food to be a crime. There is no need to prove criminal intention as a mark of an exception to the established principle of criminal liability.

But still despite all these exceptions made in favor of consumers, justice is not being delivered to them. Selling of adulterated food nowadays has become a common phenomenon. They keep becoming victim of it. No doubt for speedy disposal of consumer disputes separate consumer disputes redressal fora are established and procedural formalities are made much easier in comparison to the regular traditional courts. The consumer himself can file a simple application to seek remedy. There is no statutory requirement to engage any practicing lawyer. The complainant consumer can himself present his case before the forum. But sorry to say that large number of pendency is reported in these consumer courts, which would not be in any manner a welcome approach for the sake of administration of consumer justice.

"One may fail to understand whether it is the burden of the buyer only to testify about the quality of goods? Where the buyer has the skill to check the quality of the goods at the time of purchase? Why the rule of caveat emptor does not impose any liability on the seller to sell quality goods? Why this risk to the buyers only?"

54

Psychology of a Criminal

Criminal psychology is a kind of sickness of the mind. There should not be any doubt about it that criminal behavior in a person is an abnormal behavior. Researches reveal that the criminals are mentally sick. But the organized criminal behavior has nothing to do with the mental sickness. It is a purely professional pursuit done with a definitive intent, knowledge and awareness about the consequences of it. Whether an extreme criminal behavior has to do anything with psychological sickness of the man? Fanatic behavior amounts to be an extreme behavior and is a stage of psychological sickness. Baring exceptional situations when a person behaves criminally he has in his mind the knowledge about the nature of the unlawful act he intends to commit and its consequences as well. He also understands that the said act is prohibited by law and that he would be punished for his unlawful act.

The exponents of classical school of criminology opine that a person commits crime out of his own sweet will. He intends it and does it. The criminal plans and creates such situations and circumstances which he feels to be favorable for commission of the crime. Crimes based upon the concept of joint liability involve more than one person. Like robbery, dacoity, terrorism, waging war against state. Here in such cases the psychology of crime says that there has been an active meeting of mind of all the persons. They share the 'common intention' of all towards the perpetration of crime. They have the knowledge and are fully aware of the consequences of their criminal act. They are mentally prepared to take the law head on without bothering for the punishment whatsoever. This is very critical and dangerous psychology of a criminal when he develops a mindset where he has no fear of punishment.

There are examples of persons becoming criminal out of 'retributive tendencies.' Once they enter into the world of crime it becomes a passion for them. While the political system of a country permits its criminalization then joining politics becomes an all out attraction for criminals. Where either they support their political patrons or hijack the entire political machinery on the strength of their muscle power and money power. In contrast to the traditional crimes, white collar criminality has become a 'trend' among the persons of high social and economic status while holding public office. They have a criminal 'lust' to earn money by unlawful means to the extent possible. White collar criminal psychology has proved to be comparatively more dangerous for society than the traditional criminality and needs to be dealt with heavy hand.

"They are mentally prepared to take the law head on without bothering for the punishment whatsoever. This is very critical and dangerous psychology of a criminal when he develops a mindset where he has no fear of punishment."

55

Justice to Victims of Crime

J ustice is a concept which is not that easy to define. Legal system confers 'legal rights' and 'legal duties' to its people. Do we consider that mere enforcement of the legal rights amount to administration of justice? Or where an individual fails to perform his legal duties and by means of punishing him for his failure, the system can claim that justice has been administered? Obviously, these are very difficult questions to reply with. The most sensible question is that where the 'criminal justice system' itself fails in performing its statutory duties and functions? You can punish an individual for his wrongs. Can you punish a system for its day to day failures? Failure of system in proper maintenance of law and order in the society has been a common phenomenon. The people with criminal tendencies always take undue advantage of the system failure and these results in day to day reported instances of crime and violence in the society.

The real sufferers of these system failures are the innocent victims of crime. Had the system been alert and honest in performing its statutory functions, then it would have been in a position to prevent the crimes in the society to a considerable extent? The persons would have been saved from becoming the victims of crime. Protecting its people from becoming victims of crime or other unlawful activities is the primary duty of the State. By merely punishing the offender for his criminal act, the system should not live under any mistaken belief that it is absolved of its responsibilities. It was due to the serious laxity on part of the system that the criminal minded persons could get an opportunity to break the law and commit crimes. Who will make the system responsible and punish?

Criminal mind is very clever and culpable. Famous American criminologist Edwin Sutherland had made it expressly clear that where the situations favorable to violation of law become greater than the situations not favorable to violation of law, crime takes place in the society. Criminal mind is always ready and waits for such situations which favor it to break the law conveniently. And such favorable convenience is offered by the lax and the careless system itself. Sufferer is the poor victim for no fault of his own. The system says to the victim, look here, the offender has been punished. So justice has been done to you. Is there anybody listening to it? What made such painful situation to occur? Where is the justice? Which can hold the system responsible? Ok..! We do not expect an absolute perfection in the system but at least we do expect honest executions. If due to defective and faulty law enforcement any individual has been victimized then, let the system be punished. Punish the system. Let us have the courage to do justice to the victims of crime.

"Had the system been alert and honest in performing its statutory functions, then it would have been in a position to prevent crimes in the society to a considerable extent? The persons would have been saved from becoming the victims of crime. Protecting its people from becoming victims of crime or other unlawful activities is the primary duty of the State."

56

Criminologists and Crime

Criminologists are basically concerned with crimes and criminals. As to why do the criminals commit crimes? What are the crimogenic factors which induce criminals to commit crimes? To what extent social atmosphere is responsible for criminal behavior among people? Criminologists are more worried that we need to identify the factors which generate crime in the society. The administrators of the criminal justice should make and strictly implement policies so as to minimize the crimogenic factors prevalent in the society with a view to reduce and prevent commission of crimes.

Famous Italian criminologist Ceasare Beccaria came out with his research findings that criminals have 'hedonistic tendency' to commit crime. He is considered to be representing the 'classical school' of criminology. According to him criminals commit crimes intentionally because they derive pleasure out of it. Free will is the theory which explains that such people have a 'lust' to commit crime and by causing pain to others they feel happiness. When they are overpowered by this psychological lust they go unstoppable unless their lust for the crime is satisfied. In his book 'Crime and Punishment', Beccaria has given an elaborate explanation for criminal behavior and at the same time he further suggests the remedy through a strict punishment which 'fits' the crime. By means of inflicting punishment the criminals should be given pain so that they could be made to feel realize the gravity of the pain they caused to the victims of the crime out of their criminal behavior.

Another set of Italian criminologists is Ceasare Lombroso, Raffele Garofelo and Enrico Feri. Lombroso said that the 'criminals are born' on the basis of his plea that criminality is a hereditary character and is transferred through genes from one generation to the other generation. But in later years of his career he himself denounced his own finding and admitted that the criminals are not born but criminals are made. The three criminologists are the exponents of 'positive school' of criminological thought. Anthropological features of a person also contribute to criminal tendency. Persons with abnormal physical features suffer from inferiority complex. This induces them to commit unlawful behavior. It was discovered that persons become victims of social situations. Conflicts of these situations reach to a point of saturation. The moment saturation level of crimogenic situations crosses the limit, crime takes place. The system needs to be always vigilant enough to not to allow such points of criminal saturation in society between the rival groups to arrive at, so that the crimes are prevented.

Edwin H. Sutherland, the famous American criminologist, reveals without hesitation that the society itself is responsible for criminal behavior in persons. Society is full of diversities and is completely disorganized in the name of its vested interests. He named it the 'theory of social disorganization'. People are a divided lot in the name of caste and religion. There is acute poverty on one side for majority of people, whereas on the other side there are people who are affluent disproportionately. Such social disparities and disorganizations are the creations of society. Till such disparities exist there in the society and the system does not look for the means to remove them, make sure, crimes would continue to take place. The society could not be a crime free society. Criminals are made in the sense that the criminal behavior is learnt in the society through 'deferential association' of criminal groups. As a result of such social diversities the deferentially associated groups make crimes as their profession, for the reasons that it has its own dividends. The caretakers of the system have absolutely failed to take advantage of these researches and crime goes unabated.

"It was discovered that persons become victims of social situations. Conflicts of these situations reach to a point of saturation. The moment saturation level of crimogenic situations crosses the limit, crime takes place. The system needs to be always vigilant enough to not to allow such points of criminal saturation in society between the rival groups to arrive at, so that the crimes are prevented."

57

For a Crimeless Society?

Rule of law is the primary objective of any legal system. There should be maintenance of peace, law and order in the society. Crimeless society is the ultimate goal. Can't there be crimeless society? Criminal laws are to deal with crimes and criminals but still the society is not free from crimes. Crimes are committed in the society from time immemorial since the civilizations came into existence and are continue to be so even in modern times. Crimes have become a common phenomenon. As per the news paper reporting daily they are full with news of criminal activities. People are murdered. Women and minor girls are raped. There are reported kidnappings and abductions for ransom. Banks are looted. Thefts and extortions are committed and all around. Most dangerous criminal activities are noticed in the forms of communal violence and terrorism within and from across the borders at international levels. Cyber crimes are of the most recent origin which has broken all the limits of international boundaries. Meaning thereby with the advancement of technologies the crime techniques are also multiplied.

Whether advancement of civilizations has anything to do with the criminal behavior? Or else we are still living in the era like 'eye for an eye and tooth for a tooth'? Yes..! We claim with a sense of pride that no, we are not uncivilized. We are now living in an era of social and economic advancement. But we are not confident enough to assume that we are a crimeless society as well. Education helps in developing better sense of understanding and maturity. Understanding is a level of thinking process in human beings which enables them in distinguishing reasonably, whether what one should do and what one should not? It is always evident that an educated civilized society would always think about that what is right? And what is wrong? As to what is unlawful? What is prohibited by law? Let there be a rule of law would be the preference of the civilized society.

Are we civilized enough to see that there are no crimes in the society? Are we educated enough to ensure that there should be rule of law in the society? Whether we have developed the required maturity of understanding? If increasing rate of heinous crimes in the society today are any indications then it is evidence to the fact that we are yet to become a civilized society. Because we have failed in preventing crimes in the society. We are still a divided society on the grounds of caste, religion, language, sex, region, rich and poor. Is it due to lack of civilization, or lack of education? Divided on this line we develop our individual vested interests. We have caste considerations, religious considerations, and linguistic considerations, sexual, economical and regional considerations. These varieties of considerations give birth to 'conflict of interests' among people and communities. Conflict of interests is responsible for crimes. No matter how civilized or how educated we are? Till we are a divided society on aforesaid lines, no rule of law can stop crimes in the society. Conflict of interest on these divisions will continue to be there. At least the trend in society shows like this only. We would forget about a crimeless society.

"Understanding is a level of thinking process in human beings which enables them in distinguishing reasonably, whether what one should do and what one should not? It is always evident that an educated civilized society would always think about that what is right? And what is wrong? As to what is unlawful? What is prohibited by law? Let there be a rule of law would be the preference of the civilized society."

58

The Merchants of Death

A health hazard condition of poverty stricken masses in India is extremely painful. Poverty is a curse on human body. Proper maintenance of health needs a handsome investment. You can imagine about the people living below poverty line in worst animal like conditions. That too in an era of human rights regime. Health hazards are not only for poor but are equally applicable for rich and people in medium income groups.

In health sectors drugs and pharmaceuticals industries have grown in larger proportions. Medical treatment has become so expensive now-a-days that it is rather impossible for the poor people to get proper medication and save their life and other members of the family. Exploiting to the demanding proportions of health sectors there are spurious drugs being sold in the markets on a larger scale. These drugs are so identical that it is very difficult to distinguish between the spurious one and the genuine one. The people who are illiterate and are not in a position to differentiate between, become easy prey of such spurious drugs.

The manufacturers, suppliers and sellers of the spurious drugs are the merchants of death. They sell all these drugs to the poor innocent sick and illiterate populace. Death is being sold openly and fearlessly in the drugs and pharmaceuticals markets for a price. Instead of life saving such medicines are proving to be silent killers. The merchants of death are busy in minting money at the cost of human life without any humane consideration. It is culpable homicide well within the penal provisions of the country. I remember long time back there was a proposal in the parliament that death sentence should be the punishment for manufacturers, suppliers and sellers of spurious drugs. Unfortunately this proposal could not materialize and failed to take the shape of law. The merchants of death are at large indulging in the crime and the sin and getting scot free from the clutches of the law enforcement.

It is shameful on part of the legal administration of the country that the death merchants are not punished by the system instead they are piling up commercial gains at the cost of innocent human lives. System managers need to act tough and save the innocent. The system should understand that people are buying death for a price.

"It is shameful on part of the legal administration of the country that the death merchants are not punished by the system instead they are piling up commercial gains at the cost of innocent human lives. System managers need to act tough and save the innocent. The system should understand that people are buying death for a price."

59

Death Sentence Be Abolished?

No doubt, death sentence is a curse on the system. Sentencing to death to a person is such a painful decision for the legal system that it has become proverbial for the judge who orders death sentence breaks the nib of his pen and prays to his inner soul that let there not be a second occasion for him to order any person to death. We can understand the mental agony of the judge.

The legal systems all across the globe confer the fundamental right to life to every person in the form of constitutional guarantee. It is not only for the system but every person has to ensure that the people are not denied from their right to live. Seen in other perspectives it could be said that it is the legal duty of every person to not to deprive any other individual from his life. That is, he should not kill anybody. But bitterly speaking we cannot visualize a society which is absolutely free from crimes. Daily newspapers are full of reports with merciless brutal killings in one part or the other. Ensuring law and order becomes a big challenge for the legal system particularly under the circumstance of serious intentional violations of law for committing crimes.

Legal system would have to spring into action to stop such violations, nab the culprits and punish them in accordance with law. Punishment not only leaves a deterrent impact on the mind of the culprits but in the society as well. It is a matter of serious concern that hardened criminals have no fear of punishment in their mind. Death sentence has been provided in the penal books for heinous offences like murder, waging war against state and other related crimes of similar nature. Death sentence represents the deterrent theory of punishment whereby the criminal justice system hangs the convict to death, who has been found guilty of causing death of a person in the society. The purpose behind is to create a kind of fear of the punishment of hanging the offender to death.

After the advent of human rights jurisprudence the favorites of human rights argue that death sentence is inhuman in a developed civilized society. Therefore, they are of the view that death sentence as capital punishment should be abolished. They make anti-capital punishment campaign citing various reasons in support. There are pro-capital punishment groups also who agitate that death sentence should not be abolished and retained in the penal statutes. Because once there is no capital punishment, the criminals would be absolutely fearless of the penal system and the crime rate in the society will be high and high. For the sake of social security, therefore, the death sentence must be retained in the statute books.

Looking to the arguments and counter arguments from both the sides, it is apparent that the problem is not that easy to solve with. Maintenance of law and order is the top priority of the system through prevention of crimes. The supporters of human rights need to be equally concerned with the similar rights of the victims of crime. As per the gruesome incidence of undeterred human killings the system provides for death sentence. What will happen when death sentence stands abolished? The criminal minded persons would absolutely have no fear to kill. Certainly the system will not prefer to take such risk. Human killings would go unabated and which should not be permitted. We need to ensure that sense of social security is not endangered. Without any shadow of doubt the human rights considerations behind death sentence should be given serious thought to but never at the cost of sense of social security. The debate must go on.

"Seen in other perspectives it could be said that it is the legal duty of every person to not to deprive any other individual from his life. That is, he should not kill anybody. But bitterly

speaking we cannot visualize a society which is absolutely free from crimes. Daily newspapers are full of reports with merciless brutal killings in one part or the other."

60

The Courts- Protracted Trials

Often we come across a painful proverb 'justice delayed is justice denied'. This directly reflects upon the functioning of the courts and the machinery of the administration of justice system in the country. The pertinent question is as to why the justice is so made to be delayed? Why the justice is so denied? Who are the victims from the denial of justice? What is the legal remedy available under the system for such denials of justice? Administration of justice is not individual, it is collective. The justice delivery has to proceed through a rigorous procedural system of trial and the parties to the case are an integral part of it. Even if the justice has been delivered but after a considerable delay then such justice is of no meaning or of any use for that matter. Supposedly, where an individual knocks the doors of the court at the age of 30 years praying for the enforcement of his legal rights. Through trials in the courts below and the appellate hearings thereafter before respective high courts and then the supreme court of the country, it ordinarily on an average takes 20-30 years in final disposal of the case. There are facts to reveal that good number of cases take 20-30 years or even more to complete the hearing of the court matters at the trial stage itself. Now at the age of 50 or 60 years or even more whether the individual, even if he wins the case finally, would be able to enjoy his legal rights? No..! Absolutely not.

Undoubtedly, denial of justice is blameworthy particularly when it is deliberate. Parties to the case are to be blamed for the protracted delays. While allowing repeated adjournments on one pretext or the other put forward by the parties, the courts also become a party to the blame. The courts need to be vigilantly tough to reasonably restrict adjournments in the overall interest of the speedy delivery of the justice. There should not be any reason to forget that delay defeats the ends of justice ultimately. It should be an honest and bonafide confession that the system is laboring under the pain of a large number of pending cases before the courts for variety of reasons. The courts alone should not be blamed for this sorry state of affairs. But at the same time courts just cannot escape from their pious responsibility to ensure fair and speedy justice to the individuals particularly under the circumstances when the courts feel that the adjournment applications are moved from the parties are with an intention to delay the proceedings. A good number of vacancies are also contributory factors for piling up of court cases where the existing courts become burdened with workload. There is an unreasonable workload and at the same time quota fixed for disposal of cases by an individual court within a specified month. Then just in their bid to complete the quota courts dispose of the cases in a hurried manner. Under the circumstances it goes without saying that only judgments would be delivered by the courts and not the justice. Delivery of judgments and delivery of justice too are the two different but sensitive dimensions of administration of justice system. We have the experience of fast track courts behind. I have my own reservations whether to what extent these courts could live up to and keep track with the pious objective behind their very establishments? It needs an honest introspection.

In the modern era of human rights jurisprudence the accused are conferred with the constitutional mandate of right to fair and speedy trial. Protracted trials are bitter truths of the existing system which is not only unfair but is absolutely unconstitutional as well. If the prolonged trials for decades are concluded with by the courts that the accused found not guilty, then it is an absolute injustice for all the years of humiliation and harassment the accused has suffered due to protracted trial proceedings, just to be declared by the system that he is found not guilty. His precious life time has been spoiled completely only to know that the charges could not be proved and were baseless, he is thus acquitted of the charges by the court. Is the system is capable enough to compensate the precious days he has suffered at, with acute mental agony and harassment? Please..! Do not say to compensate the days lost in terms of money. This makes mockery of the system in the sense that we have lost control over the system which has been let loose only to compensate. There are reported instances of the under trials languishing behind the bars without trials. Whether any law on this earth would return their young hood back? Let us not argue that the system has gone sympathetic for the 'loss' and provides for compensation to them. This is no justification. The concept of compensatory justice reminds us about the helplessness of the judicial system. Compensation could be for what he has lost due to system failure but where is the justice? One thing should be made loud and clear for fair and speedy justice. That is, hang him without delay when found guilty through a reasonably fair and speedy trial following appellate procedural formalities or otherwise it should not be unreasonably protracted only to know that he was found not guilty and innocent.

It is an admitted fact that the courts have to follow a procedure established by law to conduct the trial proceedings. The courts below come across directives from higher courts that the parties should not only be given opportunity of hearing but such opportunity should also be reasonable and adequate one. It becomes a difficult and complex question of law to define an 'adequate opportunity'. Off course, it should be left up to the judicious satisfaction of the courts below, through their reasons recorded into writing. Seeking repeated adjournments by the parties could not be possible if the courts carefully examine such adjournment applications only to reject them, where in the opinion of the courts such applications are with a motive to delay the proceedings and defeat the ends of justice. The courts should avoid becoming party to such delay tactics by the litigants. It should be noted that with the passage of time and undue delay the witnesses in the cases suffer from loss of memory or they die also in due course. Sometimes they are either won over by money and muscle power or killed by the parties in interest. This is not only prejudicial to the administration of justice but the trial of the cases will linger on reducing the rate of conviction substantially. Consequently when the law breakers are out at large on the grounds of inadequate evidence, let us not expect them to be law abiding and that there will be a rule of law in the society. A society heading towards lawlessness would be a total chaos.

"It should be an honest and bonafide confession that the system is laboring under the pain of a large number of pending cases before the courts for variety of reasons. The courts alone should not be blamed for this sorry state of affairs. But at the same time courts just cannot escape from their pious responsibility to ensure fair and speedy justice to the individuals particularly under the circumstances when the courts feel that the adjournment applications are moved from the parties are with an intention to delay the proceedings."

———————————————

61

Prosecution-The Burden of Proof

The prosecution and the defense sides in the criminal trials are the officers of the court to help reach the court in administration of criminal justice. Public prosecutors represent the prosecution side whereas the defense advocates represent the accused side. They are basically advocates as per the provisions of Advocates Act, 1961. This Act controls, regulates and inculcates in them the professional ethics the advocates are supposed to follow through, a code of conduct. The fundamental requirements of the justice system is that the advocates of the two side are bound under the law to present their case before the court in such a manner that injustice is not done and the courts are properly assisted by them in pronouncement of justice.

Courts are flooded with cases with a large number of pendency. Looking to poor rate of conviction there appears to be a reason to believe that there is something wrong with the system. Increasing rate of acquittals does not mean that the defense lawyers have become extraordinary smart overnight. Poor prosecution case also remarkably contributes to this system failure. It would be a glaring painful situation where the offenders go unpunished only due to defective and poor prosecution work and ineffective prosecution proves to be abortive for justice delivery system. One should not overlook this very fact that the prosecutors have to largely depend upon the quality of police investigation with regard to proving of the case during the criminal trials. If the quality of police investigation suffers with adversities and the evidences so collected by the police do not have a concrete base then the prosecution performance cannot escape from its dismal impact during the conduct of trial proceedings in properly presenting the prosecution case. This leads ultimately to the miscarriage of justice. An acquittal after acquittals further emboldens the offenders to become professionals. They become repeated violators of law converting them to be habitual offenders. Justice system appears to be going absolutely helpless in the wake of inefficient prosecution. Police could be blamed for laxity in collecting solid evidence. But this is no way out. Who is to be held accountable after all for the miscarriage of justice? We may look for petty excuses like poor standards of police- prosecution training which negatively affects the system. I think there would not be any administrative bottleneck to improve upon such training standards. Then why to unnecessarily beat around the bush? It must be admitted with due regards that still there needs a sense of belongingness among the 'personnel' and the strong willpower to take oriented and focused initiatives for a sustainable system development.

Who makes the charge should prove first, is the general rule of burden of proof. The prosecution is to prove the case since it comes to the court with the charge sheet against the accused that is the principle. The system will not ask the accused to prove his innocence. The rule of 'presumption of innocence' proceeds on the premise that every person accused of an offence is presumed to be innocent in the eyes of law unless he is proved guilty. Where the prosecution brings the charges and the prosecution itself fails to prove it, then where is the room to question the accused? The charge goes unproved as baseless and the accused is discharged. No doubt one can say that such are the very strict principles of criminal jurisprudence which tilts somewhat to the side of the accused. But it is made amply clear that the police-prosecution is given wide statutory authority to investigate and prosecute the accused person under the law. Who stops them from quality investigations and effective prosecutions so as to get convictions under the law?

There are statutory provisions shifting burden of proof to the accused side and the presumptions of law is against the accused as well, like the cases of dowry deaths. Are we getting the desired results strictly in accordance with the spirit of law? We often come across the complaints of abuse of process of law and innocent people being victimized in the garb of presumptions of law by the caretakers of the system. It is not an ideal legal situation where there are possibilities of injustice. Can the system rule out such possibilities and ensure that abuse of process of law would not be tolerated at any cost? Can the system make a kind of declaration with full confidence that the prosecutors under the law would not 'feel' the burden but would virtually 'shoulder' the burden as desired under the law? Yes..! Hopefully the system will move on. Always there are 'silver linings' we only need focused vision to see them and follow them on honestly.

"Courts are flooded with cases with a large number of pendency. Looking to poor rate of conviction there appears to be a reason to believe that there is something wrong with the system. Increasing rate of acquittals does not mean that the defense lawyers have become extraordinary smart overnight. Poor prosecution case also remarkably contributes to this system failure."

62

Police- The Investigators

Police investigation is an important procedural legal requirement under criminal jurisprudence. In addition to its liability to maintain peace, law and order it is also the liability of the State to prevent crimes in the society. The police have been conferred with ample statutory authority to register crimes at the police stations, make investigations so as to collect evidences and get the criminals punished through court trials in accordance with law. Any criminal behavior is not considered to be against any individual but it is against the society at large, against the State. Establishment of the police system is an essential statutory function of the State. Through police machinery the State discharges its responsibility in prevention of crimes, maintenance of law and order, investigation of crimes and crime control. From time immemorial since the existence of civilized societies the criminal justice system visualizes for a crimeless society. Despite its commitments for the same the commission of crimes in the society goes unabated.

The moment any criminal act takes place in society the criminal law is put in motion with the registration of First Information Report (FIR) at the concerned police station. Police investigation starts with the registration of first information report, because on the basis of this report only police gets statutory powers to perform its function to investigate the crime. Often it becomes practically difficult for the police to pinpoint the accused or the suspects of the crime at the time of filing of this report unless named specifically by the informant in the first information. It has to depend upon the informant for crucial piece of evidence if he happens to be an eye witness. The victim surviving, the dependents of the victim or other individuals who are supposed to be aware of the facts and circumstances of the case are also very helpful for the police for the purposes of investigation.

There is every possibility that people having in prejudice with some other persons may falsely implicate their name in the FIR. The police system has to take extra caution to handle such situations and to see that the innocent are not unnecessarily harassed and the system does not become a tool in the hands of such people. It is because of these reasons that the first information report is an essential legal document in law enforcement. But it is significant to note that it has not been conferred with any evidentiary value before the courts during the trial of the cases. It can be used for the purposes of corroboration. Registration of F I R by the police is no evidence in itself to substantiate the crime. There remains a possibility for lodging of false F I Rs, thus it is no evidence. Off course, giving false information or any such implication with a prejudice amounts to serious abuse of process of law and needs to be dealt with sternly by the police administration.

Undoubtedly, collection of evidence by the police during the course of investigation is not an easy task. The criminal minds also act professionally adopting all means to destroy every possible evidence from the scene of crime. Or else they are so professional that they do not leave behind any clue or evidence for the police to collect with. It is always a painful situation for any justice system that the offenders go untraced and unpunished because of non-availability of evidence. Police training in investigating crimes is the most essential part for the police administration to be worried with. One fails to understand as to how police is not able to lift 'evidences' from the scene of the crime? Let the criminal be extra-ordinarily professional and clever but still knowingly or unknowingly he leaves behind evidence at the spot. Now it is up to the team investigators that they too are equally professional enough and clever to trace the evidences left behind by criminals and nab them. Police reaching at the spot quite late, not protecting the evidences scientifically and delays in summoning the forensic experts are some of the reported instances which adversely affect the quality of police investigations.

It is only because of lack of public confidence in functioning of the police that we often come across public agitating for transferring investigation of cases from local police units to some specialized investigating agencies. It becomes a matter of serious introspection for the police when the high courts or the apex court of the country ask the police to withdraw itself and step out from the investigation of cases. The travesty of the system is that the real culprits who are socially, economically and politically influential move scot free around while the innocent people are implicated and victimized by the police. There are instances of crimes being patronized by the system managers. Fabrication of false evidences and tutoring of professional witnesses is not uncommon in the police investigations. Complaints relating to police destroying evidences at the instance of influential people and extracting confessions from innocents under threat with a view to save the real culprits are the very serious issues which need to be urgently addressed to by the police administration. Such 'crime fixing' situations badly hit at the very root of the justice delivery system which is bound to 'miscarry' the justice. Under such situations of 'miscarriage' how can the justice be delivered that is a big question? Miscarriage of justice can be prevented provided the system managers do possess the needed determination to firmly handle with.

> *"The criminal minds also act professionally adopting all means to destroy every possible evidence from the scene of crime. Or else they are so professional that they do not leave behind any clue or evidence for the police to collect with. It is always a painful situation for any justice system that the offenders go untraced and unpunished because of non-availability of evidence."*

63

Criminal Justice Administration

Crimes are curse for any society. If the system fails to contain crimes in the society then it becomes a matter of serious concern for the administrators of criminal justice system. No doubt crimes in every society have been a challenge to the system. But despite the fact that there are criminal laws defining offences and making provisions for punishment either we are not able to nab criminals or even if we do, we fail to get them punished. The criminal justice system has a well principled approach that a person who is accused of an offence should not escape the punishment if the charges leveled against him are found proved after following the procedure established by law. Also it has to be seen by the system that under no circumstances any innocent person could be punished. Merely making a person accused of an offence does not mean that he should get punishment. Therefore, it becomes a herculean task for the criminal justice administration system to cautiously identify the culprits liable for the crime and punish them with a view to leave behind the message that the criminals would not be spared at any cost. Despite all that crimes are taking place and the objectives for crimeless society are defeated when the laws are broken and the criminals go unpunished. Still the criminal justice system struggles hard to deliver the criminal justice.

The police, the prosecution, the courts and the prisons are the four institutional pillars of criminal justice administration. Criminal justice literally means that guilty should be punished and the innocent should be protected. Every person who is accused of an offence is presumed to be innocent in the eyes of law unless he is proved guilty. Police investigating machinery is the only prevalent device to bring the criminals to book. Specialized investigating agencies of the country like Central Bureau of Investigation (C. B. I.) at Central level and Criminal Investigation Departments (C. I. D.) at State levels are working hard day and night in spotting every possible evidence through the advanced techniques of science and technology so as to get the criminals behind the bars. The police have no statutory authority under the law to punish the offenders. Still there are reported instances of police tortures and atrocities even to the innocent persons who are merely suspects in criminal investigations. Police resorting to third degree methods with a view to extract confessions is also not uncommon despite the fact that the police understand it well those confessions of the accused are no evidence in the eyes of law and are of no value during the court trials. Still the police does it on the plea that the hardened criminals won't come out with truth unless are beaten like that. The police also sometimes appear practically helpless and seem to be left with no option while dealing with hardened criminals. But this is no justification for such police deviance particularly when police forces are cornered for custodial deaths.

The prosecutors, who are the second pillar of the criminal justice system, have to further depend upon the quality of police investigation to prosecute the case before the competent court of law. It should be honestly admitted that quality of police investigation matters in proving the guilt of the accused person during the trial. At the same time it is also a fact that the police have its own institutional limitations and lack of proper infra structural facilities and training which have their adverse impact on quality of investigation. The police only are not to be blamed for that.

The courts are conferred with pious obligation to do justice with the case. Law is said to be blind but at the same time it has to very thoroughly see that whether the person accused is found guilty or not. To decide upon relevancy of evidences and admissibility of such evidences thereafter is the task to be performed by the courts. They have to appreciate the evidence as they are. The justice system has made the standard of proof 'beyond all reasonable doubts' and in case there is even a 'shadow of doubt' in proving the case then the 'benefit of doubt' will go in favor of the accused person. The standard of proof is very strict. Law proceeds on the principle with a bonafide intent to protect the innocent persons from conviction.

It is also an admitted fact that the professional offenders are taking undue advantage of this theory of benefit of doubt and getting scot free from the clutches of law. The practicing lawyers develop 'expertise' in creating doubts in the mind of the courts during the trial process through their skills of rigorous cross-examination of the prosecution witnesses. Once a doubt is created the law considers that the case is not proved beyond all reasonable doubts. The accused gets acquittal from the courts. The justice system would have to struggle hard in revamping the outdated 'theoretical dimensions' of criminal justice so as to ensure justice beyond all reasonable doubts.

"The courts are conferred with pious obligation to do justice with the case. Law is said to be blind but at the same time it has to very thoroughly see that whether the person accused is found guilty or not. To decide upon relevancy of evidences and admissibility of such evidences thereafter is the task to be performed by the courts. They have to appreciate the evidence as they are."

64

Prison Justice Administration

Prisons are the institutions where the convicts and under trials are kept by way of punishment or pending trial. Prisons serve dual purpose. Firstly, where the convicts undergo punishment after its execution and secondly, while inside the prisons the offenders are prevented from committing crimes. Prisons thus represent preventive theory of punishment. With the advent of the era of reformatory justice the prisons have become reformatory institutions. Having its preventive effect, undoubtedly till the convict was undergoing his term of imprisonment, system was able to prevent him from breaking the law. But once after completing the term he is released from the jail, there was no guarantee that he would not commit the offence again.

Crime psychology is very peculiar. Once a criminal becomes professional, crime becomes a passion for him, where he starts a well organized hardened criminal behavior. All criminals are not psychologically hardened. Many criminals are not by choice but by chance. There are many who are sensitive and emotional towards their kids and family members and repent for all that they did. Their mind boils by the feeling that they were the only bread earners for their family and they are now behind the bars for their unlawful act. Who would take care of their kids? They are put to financial hardships, livelihood sufferings and mental agonies. This is the stage when the prison authorities should take notice of it and come forward with a proper and bonafide counseling touch to their emotions. Given the chance now they are mentally prepared to respond towards a positive reformatory initiative.

There are people if we endeavor to examine, become criminals by becoming victims of the compelling circumstances and are most responsive towards reformation. Jail administration should not miss such opportunities in identifying such prisoners by resorting to the methods of 'individualization' with the help of their case history and through expert counseling treatment. Reformation of prisoners at the right moment is a crucial factor thrust upon the prison authorities. They need to ensure prison justice by properly utilizing the duration of their imprisonment. If the prison justice system makes them realize that they are being given an opportunity to reform for the sake of their family members and the kids, they would not only convert themselves being loyal to the system but also prove to be boon to the society. Let us create a kind of trust in them that the system is not after punishment only but is equally sensitive and responsive too. The fact the system well understands that had the compelling circumstances not been they would not have broken the law and committed crime.

Off late criminalization of prisons is becoming a painful trail since the hardened and organized criminals have converted the prisons into their 'dens' as 'shelter homes' and controlling their criminal activities from inside the prisons. Jail administration cannot escape from its accountability for such activities. First offenders or lesser offenders once come into contact with these 'dons' they are mesmerized with their 'glamour' and fall an easy prey to their temptation of crime world. Prison administration needs to be vigilant enough in segregating such occasional criminals from hardened ones. The jails otherwise would be converted into places transforming occasional and lesser offenders into habitual and hardened ones shattering the reformatory prison justice into pieces.

"Off late criminalization of prisons is becoming a painful trail since the hardened and organized criminals have converted the prisons into their 'dens' as 'shelter homes' and controlling their criminal activities from inside the prisons. Jail administration

> *cannot escape from its accountability for such activities. First offenders or lesser offenders once come into contact with these 'dons' they are mesmerized with their 'glamour' and fall an easy prey to their temptation of crime world."*

———————————

65

Suicide Squads and Punishment

In the existing developed and civilized society the suicide squads are posing a great challenge and dangerous threat to demolish the citadel of system of criminal justice administration all across the globe. These suicide squads are least bothered about any kind of punishment legally known in existing penal jurisprudence. Capital punishment or death sentence is the most severe form of punishment which the law can impose on an offender and deprive him from life. Death punishment is given because he has been found guilty of committing an offence under a legal system which is made punishable with death sentence. Culpable homicide i.e. killing or murdering of a human being by a human being is one such serious offence defined under the law books making provisions for death sentence for the offender if found so guilty.

Just feel the criminal psychology of the members of suicide squads. They move with a killer's instinct. Crime is passion for them. They develop their criminal psychology in such a manner that they are 'born to kill and be killed'. Absolutely no fear of punishment of death whatsoever. Modern terrorism is the dangerous concept of extreme criminal behavior. Among them the criminal psychology goes to the extent of fanaticism towards committing crimes and the suicide squads are most extreme ones. Absolutely no fear of life and no fear of punishment of any kind. They are mad after killing people brutally and ruthlessly, blood and blood around. And when they find themselves that they could be caught by the law enforcement agencies, they will ruthlessly kill themselves then and there. Even if law enforcement agencies are not around they would just complete their mission 'bloodshed' and kill themselves.

The penal jurisprudence under any legal system has its own justifications behind the infliction of punishment to the offenders who are found guilty of the committing crime by the courts of law. The penal jurisprudence considers that infliction of punishments have a deterrent effect on the mind of offenders. The various theories of punishment reveal that the objective behind the infliction of punishment is to create a fear of punishment so people are scared of punishment and do not commit crimes in the society. The preventive theory of punishment advocates that punishments have a preventive effect which helps the criminal justice system in prevention of crime in the society. Not only for offenders but it is a message for the people too in the society. The system justifies that if there is no provision for punishment then the people will never bother of committing crimes.

The justifications of penal jurisprudence have completely failed in case of such hardened criminals and the recidivists, who are the repeaters of the crime. Today crimes and criminals have acquired professional characteristics without any fear of punishment. No law and punishment under any criminal justice system of the world can stop them from committing crimes specially the suicide squads. Legal systems of the world are absolutely helpless and scared. Attack of suicide squads on World Trade Centre and Mumbai attacks are just illustrations. The administrators like America are deeply worried as to how to deter these criminals? One can understand the trauma and agony of the 'system' as laboring under pain that it has failed and it will fail to 'deliver' the justice. The crime goes unabated and the system is not able to create fear of punishment in the mind of criminals. So help us God!!!

"Just feel the criminal psychology of the members of suicide squads. They move with a killer's instinct. Crime is passion for them. They develop their criminal psychology in such a manner that they are 'born to kill and be killed'. Absolutely no fear

of punishment of death whatsoever. Modern terrorism is the dangerous concept of extreme criminal behavior. Among them the criminal psychology goes to the extent of fanaticism towards committing crimes and the suicide squads are most extreme ones."

———————————————

66

Minorities- the Respected Citizens

Who are minorities? Means who are less in number when we talk in terms of total population of any country. But the question of talking in terms of numbers whether lesser or bigger would only arise when we would see such people with the eyes of different groups. People belonging to some categories would be large in number whereas of some other categories would be less in number. Prevalent social systems divide people in different groups. In these social systems religious considerations, culture, language, script etc maintain their significant place. However, any official definition of the word 'minority' is not found but still from the viewpoint of justice administration the Constitution has made specific arrangements so that minorities get due constitutional protection.

No doubt in democratic system of any country categories like 'majority' or 'minority' matter. If any political party continuously succeeds to establish a tight grip over the majority group of the country then it will keep ruling the country. Possibly a mindset may crop up that particular parties do not need the votes of minorities and that majority votes would be sufficient enough to keep parties in power to rule the country. In such a political mindset one should not feel strange if the minority groups feel themselves to be isolated and unsafe. When 'politics' only is to be done then talks of justice or injustice to minorities goes immaterial. Such political parties would also emerge which would keep using minorities as their vote bank. They will keep frightening the minorities that they are not safe at the hands of majority groups. Make minorities believe that 'they' are the only well wishers to extend protection to them and would keep bargaining for their political motives.

Adopting judicious approach to these different groups of the society never comes within the ambit of definition of electoral politics. Their 'divide and rule' is the simple political gimmick which they better understand and befooling the different groups. Their 'show' must go on. No matter if any social group is required to be sacrificed to their vote politics. The politics of the day thus only means that such political parties would never hesitate even in giving sacrifice of these social groups just for the sake of their vested political attainment.

In Indian political scenario religion based majority or minority thinking has been much vocal and large numbers of people are not able to think beyond this mindset. What is more significant and sensible thing among majority or minority groups is that both the groups being citizens of India. When we are all respectable citizen of India then why to see them from different specs? In India either there is all politics since it being profession for the political leaders or if there is something is that day to day life struggle for the real 'majority' i.e. the common man. Poverty never looks for either caste or religion of a man. If poor people in India are large in number then who are the 'majority'? But then why should the Indian politics bother about it?

Referring to the Constitution of India Article 29 and Article 30, these provide constitutional parameters relating to protection of minorities interests. These provisions do not talk only about religion based minority but they also refer to any section of citizen who is in minority on the basis of language, script, culture. They have the fundamental right to propagate and protection of their language, script and their cultural heritage. Law of the country would help them out. Article 30 even goes to the extent that religion based and language based minorities would have fundamental right to establish and administer educational institutions of their choice for such protection. India is a country of diversities. People have diverse religious faiths, they speak different languages as a mark of reflection of their cultural heritage. Their dress, food habits and life style is also diverse but still India as a country is one. These diversities are directly linked with their dignity and identity. It is also witnessed that people from one area who are a majority in national perspectives become minority in a different particular area. But in democratic set up of the country they never compromise, at least with their identity.

It is humbly requested that 'diverse minorities' of the country should not be given an identity of 'political minority'. Minorities are the respected citizen of India, to whom the Indian Constitution has very sensibly put in through constitutional parameters, what they deserve. Justice will be done to them only when they would not be merely treated to be as 'vote banks' and could live as a respected citizen free from any fear and without any political tag.

"In Indian political scenario religion based majority or minority thinking has been much vocal and large numbers of people are not able to think beyond this mindset. What is more significant and sensible thing among majority or minority groups is that both the groups being citizens of India. When we are all respectable citizen of India then why to see them from different specs? In India either there is all politics since it being profession for the political leaders or if there is something is that day to day life struggle for the real 'majority' i.e. the common man. Poverty never looks for either caste or religion of a man. If poor people in India are large in number then who are the 'majority'?"

67

Hindu Varna System-the Untouchables

Who are untouchables? Can anyone give any official definition of untouchables? One does not feel bad if he happens to be touched by any animal. But any person from category of untouchables if happens to touch him then things go bad and the person irritates. Untouchables are also human beings but society discriminates them even to the extent of being worst than animals. Such a trend of human civilizations has been shocking and has been prevalent in Indian society. Hindu varna system has been unique in the world. Untouchables were the category of people who were not worth considered to be kept in any of the four varnas recognized in Indian society. Being considered as untouchables they were supposed to keep at a distance from rest of the people and were completely cut off and left isolated from mainstream of society. It goes beyond understanding of a common man as to what was the mindset of the society which made it so inhuman to treat its fellow human beings in such an inhuman manner.

All across the world varna system has been noticed to be prevalent in India only. In no other country of the world varna system is known to be in existence. No doubt there are reported cases of apartheid in some of the countries where there is a feeling of hatred on the basis of color of a fellow human being. Those who are fair colored establish their supremacy over blacks. There has been a trail of such discrimination in practice and Africans are worst sufferers of it. Varna system followed by caste system also attempts to establish a kind of supremacy only by way of people claiming themselves to be from higher castes. Higher castes try to keep supremacy over the lower castes putting them well below in their caste hierarchy and keep them at a distance during social gatherings or functions. The untouchables are made so also by virtue of their profession what they are 'made' to perform for the sake of their living. They will be doing the work of scavenging and cleaning human excreta, carrying on their head and that is why to be more specific they are supposed to be untouchables. All right, there is growing urbanization in India but still there are cities where lavatory and sanitation facilities are not properly available and such untouchable human scavengers are still performing the task of cleaning human excreta in these modern times. In a well informed society of today practicing of untouchability or even having a feeling of untouchability indicates for degraded civilizations.

The big question which will remain unanswered, I am sure. Whether what could have been the 'human' reason that the untouchables were left away and not considered worth to be kept in any of the categories of varna system? Was it the reason other than human existence? That is, below than the varna system categories of 'human' existence and just above than the 'animal' existence. Any justification? Despite the fact that practicing of untouchability in any form has been prohibited by the Constitution and by means of other statutory provisions, though, we do not witness this practice in open form but if we happen to go down deep in social fabric of the society feeling of untouchability is still found in the mind of people belonging to the higher caste. Laws cannot moderate 'mindset' of the people, it can only inject a sense of fear by means of introducing prohibitory measures. In an era of human rights jurisprudence now the society must show the courage to completely overhaul its mindset for betterment of human civilization. The practice of untouchability, since stands constitutionally abolished, needs to be given a 'human touch' with an honest reflection of social acceptability. We need social solidarity in every form. We need to be a strong nation without any trace of discrimination within.

"The big question which will remain unanswered, I am sure. Whether what could have been the 'human' reason that the untouchables were left away and not considered worth to be kept in any of the categories of varna system? Was it the reason other than human existence? That is, below than the varna system categories of 'human' existence and just above than the 'animal' existence. Any justification?"

———————————————

68

Fixing of Crime

Match fixing has become a very common phenomenon in the world of games. The players of the game 'fix' the match at the hands of bettors even at the cost of their national pride and the national interest. The players play for the side of their country, for which they are sufficiently paid but still the country's interest is sacrificed for petty monetary considerations. The players so 'fixed' by touts do not play their natural game 'intentionally' so as to ensure defeat of their country as per 'calculations' of the bettors. Match fixing is a serious crime. But it gets a painful thing that the managers of the 'game' fail to punish culprit players due to 'want' of sufficient evidence.

So is the case with 'crime fixing' under any socio-legal system, where law enforcement agencies are 'fixed' at the hands of organized criminal gangs. The criminal gangs perpetrate crime exactly as per their 'calculations'. Wherever and whenever they like to and in whatever manner they intend to commit crime they do. The crime fixers 'ensure' that police reaches the place of crime only when the criminals 'leave' the scene after perpetrating the crime. Crime is 'fixed' in due connivance with police. This is not only criminal and dangerous in larger public interest of any country but it is anti-national too at the same time.

The worrisome question is that whether the type of 'crime fixing' all goes on without the knowledge of the administrators of the system. It is not possible that the administrators are 'absolutely' unaware of this phenomenon. That too when it has acquired such a dangerous proportions in the system and from within the system. For facilitating perpetration of crime through 'crime fixing', law enforcement agencies are 'suitably' rewarded by criminal gangs in the form of monetary gains. Crime has become profession now-a-days as contract homicides known as 'supari' killings. Contract abductions or kidnappings are also very commonly done under protection of state agencies.

In common robberies, bank loots, dacoity etc. the robbers would commit the crime and safely leave the place and by the time police reaches to the spot, they go far away from the clutches of the law. Police reaches late at the scene of crime so as to facilitate safe escape of the offenders. Inquiries have revealed about police criminal nexus to the detriment of law and order situation in the society. The administrators need to identify the 'nexus' and deal tough and break this link at the earliest so that criminal justice system is protected by such 'touts'and to bring the perpetrators of the crime to the book strengthening the rule of law.

"It is not possible that the administrators are 'absolutely' unaware of this phenomenon. That too when it has acquired such a dangerous proportions in the system and from within the system."

69

Sentencing to Death

Sentencing a person to death is most severe form of punishment ever known in any criminal justice system. Death sentence is awarded for criminal behavior of a human being for a most serious offence of intentionally killing another human being. The logic behind this sentence is that in any civilized society every person has a right to live. The right to live is in the form of constitutional guarantee. In case an accused deprives the person from his life by murdering him then the legal system of the nations would not spare the accused and not let him to live. After completing procedural legal formalities he will be hanged to death by the system. There are sufficient reasons to justify that a person who mercilessly kills some other person, deserves to be sentenced to death. Death sentence should have a deterrent effect not only for the guilty offender but also in mind of the people in society at large. So that serious offences like murder are prevented to establish law and order. The purpose is also to reduce rate of such crimes. In human rights regime voice is also being raised now that sentencing to death is not only inhuman but it is unconstitutional as well. Therefore, it should be abolished.

Historically speaking execution of death sentence used to be very barbarous. The guilty were crushed below the feet of wild horses and elephants. Thrown before dangerous canines only to be bitten into pieces. They would be dipped live into the boiling oil tanks and fried to death. Thrown to the bottom from a high hilltop where the accused succumbs to death. He used to be beaten to death by red hot iron rods after tying him with iron pillars through iron chains. His body was cut into four pieces and hanged on four corners of the city. Hanging in full public view used to be common till very recently. There are reported instances of cementing the offenders behind the walls suffocating him to death.

Looking from the angles of human rights perspectives, no doubt such executions are anti human in a civilized society. Hanging by neck till death is the present lawful mode of execution in Indian criminal jurisprudence, but still it is objected to being inhuman. Arguments are that it is very painful to the person so kept hanging till the doctor declares him to be dead. Instead they support lesser painful modes of executing death sentence like subjecting the person to deadly injections which induce sleepy death absolutely with no pain. The caretakers of human rights are more sensitive for the rights of offenders whereas they appear to be least concerned to human rights of the victims of crime and their dependents. Perception of human rights should be equal for all. This is not the rule of law. We should not forget that the person who has been mercilessly killed and has lost his life also had the basic human right to life. State failed in its statutory responsibility to stop crimes in the society and the victim had to pay the price by losing his life for the failure of the system. It is an absolute injustice. It is agreed that we should fight for protection and promotion of human rights. But it should never be at the cost of rights of the victims of merciless crimes. The State should come forward to own its accountability to protect the human right for all. The truth is that the state has miserably failed to fulfill its accountability towards its people and thus has to pass through ordeal of losing victim's life and sentencing accused to death.

"State failed in its statutory responsibility to stop crimes in the society and the victim had to pay the price by losing his life for the failure of the system. It is an absolute injustice. It is agreed that we should fight for protection and promotion of human rights. But it should never be at the cost of rights of the victims of merciless crimes."

70

Presumption of Innocence

It is a significant principle of administration of criminal justice system that every person who has been accused of an offence would be presumed to be innocent in the eyes of law till he is proved guilty by the prosecution side. This presumption of innocence has been based upon consideration that since an offence is a crime against State, therefore, the State prosecuting agencies are given every statutory authority to get the matter investigated by the police, collect every possible evidence against the accused and then bring charge sheet before the competent trial court and get trial proceedings done. The rule of evidence prescribes that barring few exceptions it is always the burden of the prosecution to prove the case first. The legal system is not obliged to take cognizance of the prosecution charge sheet as such. Believing the prosecution charge sheet to be true the accused person cannot be asked to prove his innocence. When the prosecution prepares the charge sheet against the accused person it enlists all the evidence collected by police during investigations in support of the charges as in the charge sheet so that the court takes notice of it and proceeds with trial.

The justice system does not go by face value of the evidence produced by the prosecution side. Evidences so collected during investigation may be a kind of evidence in the prosecution's viewpoint but unless the court finds such evidences to be admissible within the parameters of evidence law it would not be taken on record as legally admissible evidence. The prosecution has to first prove to the satisfaction of the court that the charges leveled against the accused person are found established. The presumption of innocence proceeds on the foundation that when the prosecution side has brought the charges against the accused then let the prosecution prove the charges first. The accused will be presumed to be innocent for the reasons that where the prosecution fails to prove the charges then there would be no procedural requirement to ask the defense side to prove his innocence. It is for the reasons that when the prosecution itself has failed to prove the case it means it has no evidence in its possession to prove the charges. Therefore, it could be safely concluded that the charges so made by the prosecution against the accused appear to be baseless. It is only when the prosecution is able to satisfy the trial court that there are sufficient evidence in support of the charges the court will proceed to ask the accused person to put his defense and prove his innocence.

When examined minutely the rule of presumption of innocence, it would be revealed that for the purpose of administration of justice this rule imposes a kind of responsibility on the prosecution that merely making charges against any accused person would not be enough. The prosecutions would have to make honest and sincere efforts while collecting evidences during the investigation of the case. Any sort of carelessness on part of the investigating agencies at the stage of collection of evidence would prove to be damaging for the prosecution case. Taking advantage of presumption of innocence the accused person would be exonerated from any burden of proving his innocence. Justice demands that the guilty be punished. But in case where an accused could not be proved guilty and punished just for want of evidence due to 'carelessness' during collection of evidence by the police then it would defeat ends of justice. This needs to be avoided by the investigators

"Taking advantage of presumption of innocence the accused person would be exonerated from any burden of proving his innocence. Justice demands that the guilty be punished. But in case where an accused could not be proved guilty and punished just for want of evidence due to 'carelessness' during collection of evidence by the police then it would defeat ends of justice."

71

Socially Educationally Backwards

Due to social and economic conditions people remain socially and educationally backward. In raising social status money plays significant role but the people who are rich with money and a social status, does not mean that they would be socially advanced. We come across with such people who have earned money by hook or crock in all wrongful manner but they may be full with social backwardness. There are several examples of such people who lived hand to mouth and struggled in poverty throughout their life but their advanced thinking kept them always in the forefront of the society. You can well say that such people may be considered to be an exception. Similar pleas could be put forward for educational backwardness as well. Such great thinkers have also lived on this earth who never got education in any schools. Does educational backwardness mean having no school degrees? Have we not seen such society which has plenty of school certificates but still is victim of educational backwardness? Rate of literacy may be directly proportional to increasing education but the society which claims to be literate not necessary that it behaves like an educated one.

Indian social and educational backwardness is seen in link with its traditional background. Such a tradition which has a trail of social backwardness. A social group which intends to deny and see that few particular groups of society do not get proper education so that they are not able to be socially advanced. If we leave aside exceptions then there should be no doubt in accepting this fact that existing education systems of nations have a great contribution in social advancement. Yes..! If intentional bottlenecks are created in depriving off certain group of people from proper education then it is wrong and objectionable. Under such known circumstances there should not be any need to go for searching the reasons as to why we continued to be so backward socially? With an intention to bring such class of people forward and put them in the mainstream, the Constitution of India had to implement reservation system. If in even today's date the reservation policy is in force as such under the provisions of the Constitution then this is clear indication to this fact that social and educational backwardness has yet not been completely eradicated from Indian society. Had there been certain fixed time frame and the related constitutional provisions would have been enforced honestly in their true letters and spirit then there would not have been situations of differences among people in the society? The real problem lies in our attitude to keep differences, make society weak, 'divide and rule'.

This is certain that social and educational backwardness of classes in our society is contribution of Indian society itself. Then to remove it none else but the Indian society only would have to come forward. Constitutional provisions on reservation are termed as 'protective discriminations'. The moment we use the term 'discrimination' it does not sound good and one's feeling will be a bit bitter. It should be seriously prevented to happen among the social masses. The constitutional provisions instead of 'discrimination' among classes of people they need to put more emphasis on providing 'constitutional protection' to such groups. On the basis of equality of opportunity such backward classes can also come forward and join the social mainstream. By honest initiatives with absolutely no political calculations their social and educational backwardness could be removed. Ultimately society will become strong and the nation will become strong too, the social equality will be seen at large.

It is a very good sense of thing that such constitutional initiatives are being witnessed as the concept of 'social inclusions' so that honest efforts could be made to the effect that people from every class could be included in the mainstream of the nation. The time would arrive at that 'we the people of India' would say with a sense of pride that here is called the 'socialism' in true sense. The feeling of social equality is in the very foundation of our Constitution.

Social equality will prevail worth speaking only when social inequality from among people is eradicated. Let that moment be allowed to come honestly so that people from 'socially and educationally backward classes' feel it that they too are integral part of the social mainstream. Then possibly there would be no occasion for providing constitutional protective discrimination.

"The feeling of social equality is in the very foundation of our Constitution. Social equality will prevail worth speaking only when social inequality from among people is eradicated. Let that moment be allowed to come honestly so that people from 'socially and educationally backward classes' feel it that they too are integral part of the social mainstream. Then possibly there would be no occasion for providing constitutional protective discrimination."

72

L P G

This economic policy in world markets is for liberalization, privatization and globalization of world economics. There is no doubt that free market system is an indicator of economic advancement of any country. Here in this system the world countries share their free trade economic policies for mutual gains. It not only helps competition in the field of quality control of the goods but it also provides better purchase alternatives to the consumers. At the same time the consumers also get genuine price of their hard earned money. Under leadership of the countries with economic and trade technique soundness it is witnessed internationally that we have meaningful initiatives towards progress and development of world trade and commerce. The countries which are lagging behind in the race of economic advancement they have got fruitful support from such trade policies and are able to comparatively make themselves economically strong.

Globalization of trade and commerce should be understood in abovementioned reference to the advantage of progressive trade techniques from economically prosperous countries of the world should be globally available to those small and economically backward countries. These countries do possess capacity to fight with adverse circumstances, they can struggle hard but due to lack of any specific economic policy and technique they are unable to make their economic progress. The concept of globalization would be that prosperous nations of the world are in the role of 'big brother' for their economically weak nations. The advantage of trade progressive techniques need be conferred to weak nations as well. Things go wrong when strong prosperous nations go to the extent of exploiting small weak nations for their own commercial gains. They start utilizing their technical infrastructure in 'extracting' the natural resources of those nations to their disadvantage. These weak small nations are unable to utilize the natural resources to their economic interest for the reasons of their technical incapacity. Nature is full of huge resources provided we are able to properly utilize it in the interest of the economic advancement of the mankind.

Liberalization of economic policies facilitates free trading systems internationally. If we have an eye on constitution of the World Trade Organization (W.T.O.) then we come across a very specific objective for comprehensive economic strength of world nations. The world communities should come under one umbrella and other small economically weak nations should also be linked with business relations under international trade and commerce. This is a good platform for inclusive economic prosperity. When competition increases in market then according to satisfaction of the consumers and their requirements the manufacturers are compelled to maintain the quality of goods and services so that they are able to stay in markets nationally and internationally. Due to competition price of goods also becomes quite reasonable in interest of majority of consumers.

It becomes possible only when our markets and trade managers are ready to give priority to the interest of the consumers with all bonafide intentions to earn profits. The moment it appears to be going purely commercial then 'liberalization' policy clearly comes within clutches of 'privatization'. If 'liberal' economic policies of nations show their trends more for advancing in favor of 'privatizing' tendencies then this is unfair and blameworthy. It is seen that big private business houses start interfering with business policy making of nations. When few handfuls of big industrial houses are engaged in deciding so called economic liberal policies of nations in the name of privatization and globalization then one can very easily understand fate of L.P.G. It is foregone conclusion that such industrialist countries would go for their own partisan commercial benefits ignoring interest of consumers. Under these situations what the small budding businessmen would struggle to get for the sake of their business rights under free trade environment? They will be looser by all standards. Big industrialists would become stronger and stronger by taking major share of free markets while small businessmen would have to remain satisfied with whatever has been left behind. The majority of countries as such will continue to remain economically weak. We seriously need to have a relook of international trade and economic policies to search out factors as to why world trade initiatives are failing in achieving its objectives? Unless the world communities would ensure an inclusive economic and trading participation of small business nations as well it would not be possible to witness a socially and economically prosperous world.

"The concept of globalization would be that prosperous nations of the world are in the role of 'big brother' for their economically weak nations. The advantage of trade progressive techniques need be conferred to weak nations as well. Things go wrong when strong prosperous nations go to the extent of exploiting small weak nations for their own commercial gains. They start utilizing their technical infrastructure in 'extracting' the natural resources of those nations to their disadvantage."

73

Medical Ethics

Medical ethics has black spots. Reported cases of medical negligence are not unknown to the people in India. Every profession has its own professional ethics and so has the medical profession. Medical sciences confer with an expert knowledge about physiology of human body, functioning of various human organs, its morphology and diagnosis into the affected human organs with the kind of disease it could be suffering from. The practitioners would provide the remedy available under medical sciences and administer medicinal treatment to cure the disease. Doctors are given status of 'demigods' on this earth. The kind of trust people have in them is unparallel. Medical profession is service to the mankind and deserves salute of the highest order.

The 'service orientation' of medical profession has all of a sudden acquired shape of 'market orientation'. After it is deviated from path of human service it has started developing permanent black spots on its face. Now sense of devotion for the patients in doctors has become shaky in comparison to what it used to be in yester years. Yes..! We do analyze the factors behind this degradation but painfully people have no other option to refer to. Do we listen to clamoring of people that medical treatment now-a-days has become very expensive? But can't help. Those who have enough resources to refer to and avail expensive medical facilities if not the best one at least the good one, they have chances to survive. Otherwise majority of people suffering from one disease or the other die for lack of proper medical treatment. Off course the doctors only are not be blamed for such precipitating situation. In fact it is for the system managers to ensure for basic infrastructural medical facilities at grass root levels so that even poor people could afford to it. Sorry to say that the system has completely failed because of high level corrupt practices prevalent in system relating to health initiatives.

National Rural Health Mission (N.R.H.M.) could be seen as a brilliant policy initiative in positive perspectives only as a mark of concern for rural health. The people who are poor living in rural areas and are deprived of proper medical facilities. These rural health promotion policies could not reach up to the level of rural poor in need in majority of areas and the 'mission' had to collapse without completing its 'mission' due to large scale corruption among political managers, administrative officers, the doctors and bogus contractual medicine suppliers. The system managers bungled out with all money leaving aside the system as helpless moot spectator with full of tears in its eyes and looking for. If there was anyone to help it out? None comes forward to help. 'System goes like this only' was the message.

There are exceptionally good doctors in medical profession and they do have full devotion to their patients to the core of their heart. Honestly speaking, they go for only those genuine expenses for the patient whether pathological or medicinal which are just essential for proper treatment of patient. The doctors who have developed their own medical infrastructural facilities at their own cost or through borrowings in form of bank loans they have their professional limitations to charge for the expenses they have to bear on. Yes..! An honest proportion of profit also would be a necessity for their sustenance professionally.

Permanent black spots develop in medical ethics for very usual wrong reasons practiced by medical professionals now-a-days. It has gone beyond any extent to taint the entire medical community. This needs to be stopped and would be possible only when medical professionals come out firmly with a determined mind. Trading in human organs with the help of professional doctors is not only a serious issue but it is heinous crime in statute books. Kidney got removed by doctors from stomach of the patient lying senseless at the operation table is shameful by any standards. Such criminal acts have nothing to do with profession of the doctor and amount to be extreme criminal behavior holding doctors to be punished sternly. Where patient has offered his body to the doctor with full faith in him to be operated upon for the disease but instead the doctor commits betrayal of trust. It has badly shaken the 'demigod' like image of doctors among people. The kind of degradation in mindset of doctors can only be cured by doctors themselves. There is an urgent need of the society that mutual trust between the doctors and patients must be restored.

"Those who have enough resources to refer to and avail expensive medical facilities if not the best one at least the good one, they have chances to survive. Otherwise majority of people suffering from one disease or the other die for lack of proper medical treatment. Off course the doctors only are not be blamed for such precipitating situation."

74

The Peace and Brotherhood

The present society is in search of the 'peace' and 'brotherhood'. We should not feel any kind of hesitation in admitting this very fact that there is scarcity of brotherhood in society. Had there been a feeling of brotherhood prevalent in present society then merely this thing would have been enough and society would not have to deviate around in search of peace? 'Live and let live' appears to be a very simple philosophy but its deep rooted meaning needs to be understood. If there is brotherhood in society then why the society is so scattered? Why there are killings, riots, loots, bloodshed in society? Who will tell us after all, whether what is good or what is bad for us in our larger social interests? We do not understand that any 'angel' will come from space down to earth only to tell us from time to time that what is good or what is bad for us? And also to tell us that what should we do for maintaining peace and tranquility in society? And not to do those acts which amount to breach of peace in the society? We should also not expect at the same time from so called social leadership that just by talking to 'peace' and 'brotherhood' they would liberate us from our problems. If there is no problem in society then they are left with no work. They need work so there remain problems for them to keep working on it. Who will then approach to them? They cannot think of a society with peace and brotherhood. They are virtually the problem makers, create breach of peace in society and are 'traders' of polluting the atmosphere of brotherhood in and around. In search of peace and brotherhood the society would ultimately keep working for these traders. The traders would not take any guarantee for establishing brotherhood in society but yes they would keep making efforts for it and recover 'price' from people in exchange. Where there is some deficiency for the desired price they will see to it.

Proper education in society better makes one to understand about good and bad for them. It is a matter of serious concern that even today a majority of public continue to be uneducated. This is a system fault and which is not good for social health. But when we talk about even completely uneducated person he too has a natural consciousness about goodness or badness of things for himself. For such natural consciousness we do not need any schooling. Even if society is uneducated then pertinent question is where the natural consciousness of people gone? Who will ever like to lack of peace, brotherhood and commission of killings, riots, bloodshed in society? Who would not prefer to that there should be brotherhood? Sensibility and feeling of brotherhood is nature born and for it we the society do not need any school certificate. The day society will make a kind of determination to the effect that establishing peace and brotherhood is their personal matter. That they have to live with the feeling of peace and brotherhood in society. That in this living lays their 'comprehensive' interest. Such message only from society would be enough to 'convey' to these traders and would thrash out their malicious intentions.

Well organized and strong society is need of the day. With the help of this social strength the traders would be deterred and not be successful in their ulterior motives. It is unfortunate that poverty and lack of education in our society weakens the process of social organization. This only is the weak chain which affords an opportunity to these traders to creep in our social fabric and then successfully come out with their malicious agenda. May be people in our society are alert to the greatest extent that they only would worry for their good and bad and that they will continue to remain in depravity but the peace and brotherhood would be their top priority. They would not compromise with and never accept any interference from these traders. But the moment they and their kids would feel the punch of poverty and hunger their consciousness of peace and brotherhood would collapse then and there. They are forced to surrender and compromise. Peace and brotherhood has to give way.

It should be our prayer to the Almighty that our society be liberated from the curse of poverty immediately. Even if the society is weakened by poverty but still by and large society is peace loving. It is the 'traders' who keep fuelling and disturbing maintenance of peace reaping harvest for their future political gains. Alright. Accepted that no system has any such 'machine' to eradicate poverty. Doing hard labor could be the only alternative. But one fails to understand about the 'machine' which converts the assets of corrupt system managers into millions overnight. Keeping people in society poor and weak appears to be the clear policy of the system. Their 'trade' would flourish in a society which keeps demanding for peace and security. Point to consider is that society itself would have to take initiatives to remove poverty without blindly depending up on system. The caretakers of system are expected to sincerely come forward by creating favorable opportunities through honest and determined breakthrough. Society suffers moral hazards in witnessing lack of brotherhood even between two real brothers. To overcome these hazards would be job of society itself. No way out whatsoever. It is definite that an organized and strong society would on its own be in a position to establish peace and brotherhood for itself. Do not forget that this society has the required optimism and that it shall do.

"Alright. Accepted that no system has any such 'machine' to eradicate poverty. Doing hard labor could be the only alternative. But one fails to understand about the 'machine' which converts the assets of corrupt system managers into millions overnight. Keeping people in society poor and weak appears to be the clear policy of the system."

197

75

Preventive Justice

Preventive justice and prevention could be two different things. From the view point of administration of justice in society and examining the linking with the proverb 'prevention is better than cure', preventive measures are most effective in establishing maintenance of peace, law and order in society. Law enforcement agencies are given with the task to enforce preventive laws. The policing system if accomplishes its statutory responsibilities with due honesty, integrity and accountability then there is no reason for any lawlessness in society. It is never maintainable that police should wait for the crime to happen and then switch over to punitive measures of legal administration. The proverb is well said in the sense that our 'human body' has its own mechanism. If we do not take proper care of the mechanism and its other various parts then they are amenable to develop defects and it would adversely affect entire system of human body. We then refer to cure the disease through treatment. Curing could be a lengthy process depending upon nature of defect. The defect could be of serious nature if degree of 'carelessness' was on higher side. It is always dangerous letting a disease to be incurable, since now it will not be localized in particular area only but will spread over the entire system with imminent system collapse. System collapse defeats the ends of justice if seen through social perspectives. Prevention is rigorous and continuous process. It cannot be practiced in parts or at intervals. It needs an alert mind with fine perceptive capacity to strike with. A careful observation of chain of events would enable system managers to understand as to what could be the exact preventive step. It would be significant to stop the defect to creep in the system.

It goes without saying that adoption of preventive measures is a state of mind. An alert mind always ensures prompt and powerful action to counter with the ensuing problems. It should always be a matter of serious concern as to how much alert our legal enforcement is? How carefully do we prepare our action plan whenever we come across any 'chain of events' indicating for an immediate strike? We have in system well knit intelligence machinery but still law enforcement machineries are not able to strike timely and prevent crimes in society. What do we conclude then particularly when our society comes across more serious crimes like communal riots, waging war against state, and well calculated terrorist attacks? Our intelligence agencies do not carefully watch the chain of events happening across in society or by the time they respond to such situations, it goes too late for enforcement of law to strike with at the right place and at the right moment of time. It is also seen that despite timely response by intelligence, laxity and inaction on part of law enforcement proves abortive to strike any effective preventive measures ultimately giving rise to failure of system and defeating objective behind prevention. Administrators of system are advised to go for preventive steps in advance rather to keep working for cure and treatment. A system which has failed to develop its preventive mechanism and is kept subjected to treatment and cure is said to be a weak system. When the ailment goes incurable for carelessness on our part then it is considered to be not good for social health.

Honestly speaking we cannot claim to be an absolutely crimeless society but when we register increasing rate of crimes like 'collective violence' one is forced to think about lack of co-ordination and a kind of communication gap between the intelligence and the law enforcement. We need to give a serious thought to it otherwise our 'preventive mechanism' will be destroyed. Keep depending on cure is not always good for system. For lesser crimes the law enforcement needs to develop its own intelligence may be less professional but more effective.

"An alert mind always ensures prompt and powerful action to counter with the ensuing problems. It should always be a matter of serious concern as to how much alert our legal enforcement is? How carefully do we prepare our action plan whenever we come across any 'chain of events' indicating for an immediate strike?"

76

Lokpal- the Indian Ombudsman

Looking to gravity of corruption in India institution of 'lokpal' could be a necessity. Corruption is as old for Indian society as has been the independence from British regime. Our political system has accepted it as a global phenomenon. If rest of the world could not fight with corruption then how can we the Indians? Such arguments could be given. Recent socio-political developments on issue of institution of lokpal have made it an instrument of political reflections.

Ombudsman is of western origin and to a considerable extent it has made its impact felt to deal with vices of corruption in those countries so far. We the Indians feel more comfortable in 'following' rather than 'leading' one. Since we were under British for centuries, they ruled over us by laws made in British parliament. After independence we never felt any hesitation in adopting the same British legal system to which we used to object to, when it was enforced against us by them. Now India is being ruled by Indians following the same British legal system. Ombudsman cannot be an exception to it. Here the lokpal or lokayuktas i.e. Indian ombudsmen are already in action. But we do not come across any such notable illustration that they have left any impact to deal tough with corruption. They have proved to be more political 'accommodations' rather than serving institutions for the burning cause. While following and adopting any 'western' or 'eastern' model we forget that they are honest, laborious, dedicated and have a sense of belongingness for their nation. They individually and collectively live for their nation and die for their nation.

Japan was completely destroyed after nuclear holocaust over Heroshima and Nagasaki (1945). Now today they are far ahead of us. After we got independence (1947) where we stand today? Yes..! We should admit this bitter truth that we were not 'honest' to our nation's growth during all these years. The result is that we are lagging far behind marred by corruption all around. Indications are that it is not going to stop in near future. Issue of nation's growth would definitely be of grave concern.

Lokpal versus janlokpal has been the recent political controversy. Instead of making it controversial the nation's interest should have been on top of the agenda by either side. Whether it happens to be a lokpal or janlokpal how does it make the difference? The serious issue of corruption is more preferably to be addressed to. The mindset of caretakers of system and of the people abetting for indulging in corrupt practices needs to be reoriented. Would the lokpal or janlokpal prove to be a panacea? Certainly not. After all they would also be from among human beings only with a human mind. Don't expect them to act like angel supernatural. They too could be amenable to 'inducements' under the circumstances. They are bound to commit 'human errors' leading the institution of lokpal towards complete collapse. Let we the Indians come forward collectively with a mindset to prove that it is not always destiny of the Indians, we too can.

> *"Now India is being ruled by Indians following the same British legal system. Ombudsman cannot be an exception to it. Here the lokpal or lokayuktas i.e. Indian ombudsmen are already in action. But we do not come across any such notable illustration that they have left any impact to deal tough with corruption."*

77

Maintenance of Peace Law and Order

Every society has the basic concern that there should be maintenance of peace in society. We the people of society would also have to take a determination to make peace in society with the help of rule of law. If maintenance of peace is disturbed and laws are broken in society who will be the sufferer after all? Undoubtedly..! The people in society only would be sufferers. Majority of sufferers would be of those in society who have no say in the system and who have no reach in the system. If few of 'them' could any how manage to 'reach' to the system still nobody listens to them and by the time it is 'too' late.

See..! We the people of society need to understand this fact in a proper manner that we are also equally responsible and duty bound to see that there is maintenance of peace, law and order in society. In India it is general perception and that is found to be true also that 'communal riots' do not take place in India but they are 'made to happen' and 'managed' by forces with partisan socio-political interest. Where there is no management in system politics makes its safe entry into it. Every 'politico' develops his own vested interest in terms of 'profits' and 'loss' to their vote bank. It is fix and goes without saying that peace of society has to be 'sacrificed' now at the cost of political calculations of these politicos.

Why to talk about Indian society only. In other societies too there is no scarcity of antisocial elements. They are easily available to politicos, do their job and take price for it. They are least bothered about peace in society. On the other hand, if there is maintenance of peace in society on its own then they will lose their source of earnings? If there is no 'heat' of disturbed peace, no 'heat' of riots, how the politicos would be able to 'cook' for themselves? And possibly the 'politicos' in nexus with 'antisocial' elements are so spread around in society that they would never like that their 'shutters' are closed down. The system has evidence to the fact that such antisocial elements are professional active workers of these politicos only. What is painful is that despite all such evidences, the system sits with its fingers crossed and some way or the other system goes 'slave' in the hands of and under the 'influence' of politicos. What would you expect from a slave? Would he be able to do his jobs with full freedom and strength? Had he been 'that' powerful then why would he gone a slave? For the sake of maintenance of peace, law and order we the people of India 'need' to have answer of these questions from 'caretakers' of system.

That antisocial elements would go essentially to disturb maintenance of peace or for communal riots, it is not necessary. This would simply serve their purpose if they are able to 'create' a kind of fear of 'breach of peace' or fear of 'out breaking' of riots in mind of the people. This itself would be 'sufficient' to keep their 'shutters on' because on the strength of this fear itself the politicos antisocial nexus would keep 'harvesting'. The fear deep in mind of the people is not without reason because they do know that the 'hands' which are supposed to extend 'protection' to the people under the law, are far from law and maintenance peace are busy doing slavery of the politicos.

As on today, if all is not well in India then it has its own solid grounds. We are not ready to treat it as any compulsion of the system. If we have strong 'determination' and a little bit of 'will power' then what else we are supposed to think about and do? We talk about the law and have to establish the rule of law. That's it. Is there any system in this world which discourages the initiatives for rule of law? Or questions about the system managers? Possibly none. Then what for slavery? Laws are made by legislative bodies of our country and under rule of law these law making institutions are our strength. Who would be able to stop us from maintaining peace, law and order in society? And from establishing the rule of law? Yes..! Nobody can but subject to the condition that the 'firm determination' and the 'will power' we need for it, has to be created by us only within ourselves.

Keep depending blindly on system managers only would be a big mistake. The people in society cannot escape from their liability to keep peace. Law will come into picture only later when there would be a law and order problem. This has to be ensured by society itself that people live with sense of togetherness and mutual respect so that there is no 'occasion' for disturbance of peace. Antisocial elements and dishonest politicos be exposed_with brotherly co-operation of people in society. Law is able to work honestly provided people themselves in society are alert for their comprehensive social interest and their protection. No antisocial element or politico would be able to dare to disturb peace, law and order. By means of winning over the fear society would gain health and strength from within.

"The people in society cannot escape from their liability to keep peace. Law will come into picture only later when there would be a law and order problem. This has to be ensured by society itself that people live with sense of togetherness and mutual respect so that there is no 'occasion' for disturbance of peace. Antisocial elements and dishonest politicos be exposed with brotherly co-operation of people in society. Law is able to work honestly provided people themselves in society are alert for their comprehensive social interest and their protection. No antisocial element or politico would be able to dare to disturb peace, law and order."

78

Terrorism All Around

What do we mean by terrorism? Literally it goes like that a kind of extreme behavior which creates terror in mind of the people. Terror creates fear consciousness and an extreme sense of fear relating to safety of life of the person and his kith and kin. It also relates to safety of properties belonging to people which they have earned by putting hard labor through out their life. This behavior becomes more dangerous when it is used as a 'tool' following political motivations. In modern world the extremism could be witnessed in the form of international implications. The extremists have their own agenda to settle with in the arena of international politics. The extreme behavior could be seen in the form of collective violence causing huge loss of life and property to innocent people.

In the present era terrorism has become professional. Political or administrative bosses are seen resorting to 'terror' to get the work done strictly for the sake of their own vested interests. It may appear to be a 'revolutionary' approach if such 'terror tactic' has been opted out by these masters with a view to secure performance, transparency, enforcement and disposal in larger public interest. India has witnessed continuous failure of poverty eradication programs since independence. Had there been a 'terror' mode in policy implementation of the governments then definitely India would have achieved much satisfactory progress to reckon with regards poverty eradication. Needless to say those human development policies apart from poverty eradication like basic education and primary health are sulking under the pressures of defective decision making followed by not so smart enforcement. Here India needs the real 'terrorism' on part of governors so as to create terror and secure honest 'enforcement' of policies which could appear to be smart enough provided if the people in need are actually benefitted by these policies terror is justified. It is an absolute lack of terror only that enforcement is badly marred by large scale corruption on part of public officials and so called developmental policies succumb to administrative and political inaction. People are reminiscent of the days during 1975-76 when emergency was proclaimed in India. People do not forget that it was the 'terror' of emergency only that the administration sprang into action mode and upright. Things started getting worst just after since democratic India voted against it only to repent thereafter.

Indian judiciary justifiably interferes with in situations of administration inaction and where it comes to its notice that there is violation of rule of law. No doubt this may not appear to be in good taste. Critics refer to 'active' judiciary as 'judicial terrorism'. But after all what is the way out? They will not deliver the 'good' unless they are put in terror and they will 'bungle' out with the things if they are given a sort of liberty. It is not good for Indian destiny. Feeling of delivering well should come to us from within and not out of terror. Let us not make it known to others that we are in habit of doing well only when we are put to terror. Possibly our mentality like these stops our nation India from approaching forwards. It is the time that first we do justice with us, understand our duty and be honest to ourselves. The terror would not frighten us then.

"Needless to say those human development policies apart from poverty eradication like basic education and primary health are sulking under the pressures of defective decision making followed by not so smart enforcement. Here India needs the real 'terrorism' on part of governors so as to create terror and secure honest 'enforcement' of policies which could appear to be smart enough provided if the people in need are actually benefitted by these policies terror is justified."

79

No Miscarriage of Justice?

Pregnant with justice? There should be no miscarriage of justice? If all goes well then 'justice' must be delivered? Justice delivery is very delicate and sensitive. System must be taking all due care and precaution for 'safe' and 'successful' delivery of justice? People must be full of joy and celebrations when they would be thinking about justice? As to how the 'justice' would be and looking like after it takes birth? They just imagine. It must be sound, healthy, and hale and hearty. They cheer with joy!!! The most awaited moment has arrived at ultimately. Since it is the day when 'justice' is going to be 'delivered'.

Justice delivery used to be so simple in ancient times, they think. But today they appear to be full of 'anxiety' and 'nervousness' regarding safe delivery of justice. Their concern is quite genuine. They are told that in modern times the justice system has been well equipped with advanced research and development in the fields of legal sciences. Legal sciences have developed techniques to 'diagnose complications' during the various stages of 'pregnancy' so that by timely resorting to proper treatment, complications are done away with. And the system is able to successfully 'prevent' any chance of 'miscarriage' of justice. They are also told to their surprise that 'law clinics' are at work 'round the clock' to promptly attend to the cases with serious complications to provide 'intensive care' and 'clinical attention' to ensure with proper delivery of justice.

They remember that in old days they were 'unaware' of any such complications during justice delivery. Modern 'researches' and 'developments' in the field of legal sciences have made them more 'apprehensive' relating to the complications during 'pregnancy' stages of delivery of justice. They are scared as well. What will happen if complications turn to be serious enough and may cause 'miscarriage' of justice? The mere imagination of miscarriage of justice 'moves' them from within. What this system is all about? They retort mixed with fear and anger. How does these complications in justice delivery system? Who permitted them to 'creep in' and make space? There should not be any 'space' for complications in justice delivery. Right is right and wrong is wrong. That's it. Once a right always will be right. Where is the room for complications then? Go for the right and let the justice be delivered. There is no reason to allow the matters to be serious and be burdened with complications and 'referring' them to 'law clinics' for treatment just in a desperate bid to prevent miscarriage of justice. Complications would prove to be 'abortive' leading to no delivery of justice.

The aforesaid story presentation may appear to be quite imaginary, strange and undeliverable. Right from my childhood I have heard about justice to be delivered only. The reasoning mind goes on to argue that if the system is 'pregnant with justice' then justice only will be delivered. What else..? What will happen if the system is not pregnant with..? No delivery. Justice delivery must be a 'natural process' of law. When we talk about the natural process of justice delivery, the 'period of gestation' promptly comes to my mind. This is a creation of the nature. During the period of gestation the material acquires its 'shape' only to follow the process of delivery after the gestation period is complete. Things go beyond the control of experts in case 'rule of gestation' has not been followed and grossly violated. Miscarriage or forced 'abortion' would be the result of such violations, just in a bid to save life of the system. Where pregnancy prolongs 'beyond gestation' it will prove to be dangerous to the entire system and the expert 'law clinics' would not be in a position to help it out.

If we would go away from the nature we would not be able to survive on this earth. Same is applicable with justice delivery system as well. We need to give a serious thought to it and take definitive measures to prevent miscarriage of justice. Justice delivery prolonging for years and years even for justifiable reasons would be against the nature and in violation of the 'rule of gestation'.

It would be definitely amounting to justice miscarried. Let the system ensure that the justice does not prove to be abortive for the reasons of violation of 'natural process' of law. The legal system has prescribed 'limitation' to complete hearing of the cases well within defined statutory time limit. That's the 'gestation period' in the legal system. Does the system follow to deliver justice within prescribed limits? The answer will be in negative. It could be very easily understood then as to what would be the fate of delivery of justice? It is very rare that court cases are decided within the prescribed 'gestation period' of limitation as under the law. This must be painful. The justice delivery system may appear to be 'pregnant with justice' but 'miscarriage of justice' is bound to happen for the factors of 'gestation' limits violations. If such 'violations' are much larger in number, which the system is well aware of, let the system talk to its 'inner conscience' about the 'kind' of justice to be delivered.

> *"We need to give a serious thought to it and take definitive measures to prevent miscarriage of justice. Justice delivery prolonging for years and years even for justifiable reasons would be against the nature and in violation of the 'rule of gestation'. It would be definitely amounting to justice miscarried. Let the system ensure that the justice does not prove to be abortive for the reasons of violation of 'natural process' of law."*

80

Ready to Kill and be Killed

In present criminal world there are criminals who are ready to kill and be killed after committing crime. It has proved to be extreme criminal behavior with extreme criminal psychology. They are the biggest challenge in the history of world crimes. If we go by legal procedure then where a person is accused of criminal behavior and has been proved guilty under criminal justice system the system convicts him and awards him punishment as per the gravity of the offence as defined under relevant penal statute. The gravest offence under the criminal law statutes is 'culpable homicide'. The gravest form of punishment recognized under criminal statutes is death sentence.

The philosophy of criminal justice system is that when any person violates the law and commits crime then he should be punished for his wrongful act. Awarding punishment is also at the same time a message to the society at large to make people not to break laws. But worry of system is that recent trends of this extreme criminal psychology 'ready to kill and be killed' has started 'deterring' the entire criminal justice system itself all over the world. But the system is not getting the desired result of awarding punishment to deter criminals with this extreme criminal psychology. They are being termed suicide squads. It is extreme criminal behavior in the sense that they absolutely do not care for their own life.

Problem of legal system becomes more serious because the system fails in stopping them and laws are broken the way these criminals like to. They go for certain bloodshed and are ready to kill themselves as well after committing the crime exactly according to their calculations. They take the legal system and law enforcement administration head on. It's a war of such criminals straight with the criminal justice system itself. They are least bothered about the law, the system and the justice. Once they target for the crime they are unstoppable by law let there be any punishment whatsoever. Even if they happen to fail to commit their intended crime due to alert law enforcement they will ensure to kill themselves with a view to surely avoid to get caught by the police.

It would be my humble submission at this stage that system needs to conduct a thorough study into situations and the circumstances of such persons becoming extreme criminals to the extent of ready to kill themselves for the crime. Do we ever find time to think about them as to what made them to go so extreme? It should be a matter of serious concern for administrators of the system to think about and know as to why these criminals went cut off from mainstream of social world? We should not forget that no person is a born criminal. They are also human beings only and could be reformed. The system should always keep hope and not make any final opinion that they are incorrigibles. They could be well reformed and brought back into mainstream of society provided we make honest initiatives in that direction and handle their psychology with a 'caring' hand.

"Do we ever find time to think about them as to what made them to go so extreme? It should be a matter of serious concern for administrators of the system to think about and know as to why these criminals went cut off from mainstream of social world? We should not forget that no person is a born criminal. They are also human beings only and could be reformed. The system should always keep hope and not make any final opinion that they are incorrigibles."

81

Justice Delayed and Denied Too

We talk a lot about fast disposal of court pendency but practically it does not appear so. There happens to be a large pendency in courts and that is the truth also. Delay in justice defeats the ends of justice. When the purpose of justice itself gets defeated due to delay, then there appears to be no need to merely follow the procedural formalities just in the name of justice. In lower courts and higher courts as well the matters are lingering for long periods. The very problem lies in the fact that courts are bound to follow the legal procedure for completing hearing of cases. If without fulfilling all procedural formalities hearing of cases have been completed then very validity of hearing process itself is put in question.

A principal factor which is said to be a reason for delay in judicial process is that procedural laws are very complex. But there appears to be no much force in these arguments. If we go deep in procedural laws then we would find that these laws are purely based upon the principles of natural justice only. Opportunity of hearing has to be given to every party to the case whether it is a quasi-judicial process or completely judicial. It is very difficult to give a specific definition as to when and what amounts to be an opportunity of hearing? Where opportunities of hearing are already given to the parties concerned then the appellate court may 'stay' the order given by the courts below on grounds that 'sufficient' opportunity of hearing was not given. Some well defined parameters are determined and by measuring out on such parameters courts could satisfy by the fact that the parties to the case have been given 'opportunity' of hearing. Matters should not be kept delayed further and hearings of the cases are completed.

Laws are not complex. Complexity in fact is in our mind. Agreed we make the laws simpler the way it is argued. But how to remove the complexity of the minds? Laws are not of divine origin. We only sit together and make laws for ourselves. When there is 'complexity' in our mind itself then the laws would automatically become complex. Unless sincere efforts are made to simplify these 'complexities' delays are bound to take place in justice administration. In our procedural laws clear emphasis has been made for time bound disposal of cases by courts but still there use to be considerable delay in hearing of cases. Such delays take place not only in trial courts below but before appellate courts also it takes long time in final disposal of cases. Adjournments in hearing of cases are the most common factors in delaying hearing of cases. Such 'pending' matters also come into notice where trial court or any quasi-judicial authority has completed hearing into case and has delivered its judgment. The matter goes in appeal. The appellate court is also satisfied with this fact that an 'opportunity' of hearing was given but since in the opinion of the appellate court an 'adequate' opportunity of hearing was not given to the person, the appellate court grants stay order against the judgment of the trial court or the quasi-judicial authority and the matter is left pending for many more years to come. This is very common. Under such conditions undoubtedly the purpose of justice gets defeated.

In majority of cases the 'parties' themselves one way or the other 'manipulate' the matter to see that cases remain pending. They feel it is in their interests. Law makes it expressly clear that 'malicious' delays in disposal of matters should never be permitted. Matters are left pending for decades and decades. With passing of time many eye witnesses either die their natural death or they are murdered. Their memory also starts fading away and they are not able to remember or connect the chain of past criminal incident. Then there is no meaning of their evidence before the law. Contradictions are bound to be there. Benefit of contradictory circumstances straightway goes in favor of the accused persons. Here comes a big question mark on procedural system of justice administration. Whatever adjournments are to be permitted it is with permission of the courts only. If courts reject such malicious adjournment applications by a speaking order then there must not be any reason that court hearings are not completed well within time.

The courts need to be strict in this regard. It should always be kept in mind that it has become proverbial that litigants only go to courts to take the next date in the case. The next date in the court cases is usually granted not by the court but by the court clerk only. Litigants could be seen bribing court clerks for an early date into the matter. It goes on like this only. Advocates are also more interested in adjournments rather than hearing and timely disposal of cases. Ultimately it is for our justice system only which would have to take tough initiatives in this direction that due to 'delay' in administration of justice the people are not 'deprived' from justice.

"Laws are not complex. Complexity in fact is in our mind. Agreed we make the laws simpler the way it is argued. But how to remove the complexity of the minds? Laws are not of divine origin. We only sit together and make laws for ourselves. When there is 'complexity' in our mind itself then the laws would automatically become complex."

82

Are You Innocent?

At least you only know that what is the truth? You only know that you are innocent or not. It is very rare that an accused person or a person doing a wrongful act admits that he has done that wrongful act. Even a murderer who is responsible for a cold blooded murder, that too he knows this fact, but still he always claims himself to be innocent during the entire legal proceedings. Where the accused desired to take legal advice for his unlawful act then also he is advised by his lawyer that he has to claim himself to be innocent only. Rest will be 'seen' during the trial of the case. Despite the fact that advocate knows that his client only is behind the crime but still advice is like that only. After all the accused also after committing any crime only requests to his advocate that he be saved.

Legal procedure offers every accused person an opportunity to put his defense. The very honest and pious purpose of this procedure is that an opportunity of defense is to be given for the reasons that it should be made sure that innocent persons should not be punished by making him an accused. Definitely but not for the reasons that the person accused who knows that he has intentionally broken the law and has committed crime, should use this procedure of opportunity of defense in his favor just to prove him to be innocent. Should this not be treated as abuse of the process of law? Particularly when evidences are manipulated to the extent of destroying them for proving innocence. Who knows that the accused is innocent? Without doubt..! The accused himself. But he is not ready to accept his guilt and he has been given the legal advice like this only. Make this a point that ours or any legal system of the world does not have any 'magic stick' just to move it round only to know the truth whether the person before it is guilty or innocent.

Legal systems too have to be completely dependent on those facts only which crop up during trial by either party to the case. These facts only the legal system recognizes to be evidence. It is not a new thing for the legal system to know that parties to the cases do not 'create' evidences or 'manipulate' with evidences. They do it. False evidences are made, witnesses are tutored to speak false during trial before the court. Such ways and means are 'searched' by parties to the cases only for reasons that accused persons could be 'proved' innocent. By this manner the purpose of legal procedure is put to manipulative exercises only to thrash away the ends of justice.

Our legal system also cannot 'justifiably' claim it that it remained completely 'unaware' about all that happenings during hearing of the cases. It could not sense that the trial proceedings were unnecessarily prolonged. That there was a gross abuse of opportunity to prove innocence by the accused persons. And that the caretakers of the system could not also visualize that ultimately justice only was going to be defeated. Even if the system was 'aware' about all that it had no means to stop it. There are completely two different things. Firstly, that there was clear evidence to 'prove' that accused was 'innocent'. Secondly, due to lack of evidence the accused was 'presumed' to be innocent. In the larger interest of justice responsibility is entrust upon the justice system to minutely examine both these situations. There are clear evidences for accused being innocent meaning thereby the justice system is fully satisfied about innocence of the accused. Under such circumstances the justice system comes out with a definitive judgment. But where there are situations of doubt, it was not being proved that the accused was guilty but there was no concrete evidence either to prove him innocent. The system goes for allowing benefit of prevailing situations of doubt to be given in favor of accused and letting him go by 'treating' him to be innocent.

There is a clear scope of abuse of process of law. It is very easy task to make an 'artificial' situation to show that evidences are 'lacking' or evidences not being 'collected' honestly against the accused. Prevalence of nexus between parties is not an unknown thing for the legal system. Even if the legal system has knowledge about this 'nexus' then what it can do? It cannot help. It has been made 'blind' with its eyes tightly covered. How could it see all that nexus? Who knows that the accused is innocent? The accused has not to do much to bring any particular evidence to prove his innocence. He has to just raise certain facts during the hearing of the case that it produces a situation of 'doubt' in the mind of the law. That is all. Several such 'legal advice' is made available in the course of legal profession by its professionals. What is the need to bring forward the truth? Situations of doubt are to be made and the accused is to be let go by treating him to be innocent. Where in a justice system, situations of doubt are allowed to make a dominating and deciding factor than perhaps it is most unfortunate for justice administration system. Let the Almighty help us.

"Prevalence of nexus between parties is not an unknown thing for the legal system. Even if the legal system has knowledge about this 'nexus' then what it can do? It cannot help. It has been made 'blind' with its eyes tightly covered. How could it see all that nexus? Who knows that the accused is innocent?"

83

Why to Blame the Legal System?

Amidst claims and counter claims between government 'lokpal' and 'jan lokpal' all across country has been passing through a struggling phase. It must be considered to be a happy indication that 'we the people of India' are not all indifferent towards serious problems of Indian society. The people have started accepting that public life corruption in India is getting cancerous. According to medical sciences 'cancer' is incurable. If we wish to save our Indian nation and its democracy before it is too late, we need to cut and remove the affected parts by 'cancerous' growth. Otherwise it will 'spread' in entire Indian democratic system resulting to system collapse. It is not like that in India there were no laws to deal with 'ailment' of corruption. The Prevention of Corruption Act 1947 was the principal law which was later repealed and replaced by more 'stringent' Act of 1988. Act of 1988 was claimed to be comparatively more comprehensive and effective law to handle out corruption. To ensure speedy and thorough investigation of matters relating to corruption 'special police establishment' was constituted under Delhi Special Police Establishment Act 1946. For expert investigation of corruption related matters arguments were introduced to provide scientific and specialized training to this police establishment so as to ensure highest level of quality investigation. Motive behind was expressly clear that concrete piece of evidences should be collected after comprehensive investigation against corrupt ones and they should be duly punished in accordance with law.

In due course on the lines of American Federal Bureau of Investigation (F.B.I.) the Indian special police establishment came to be known as Central Bureau of Investigation (C.B.I.). I still remember on being questioned by journalists our responsible people's representative heard making statements that 'corruption is a global phenomenon'. Do we mean by it that to prevent corruption in our society is almost not possible on mere pretext that it is a global phenomenon? That's why we are helpless? And that tendency of corruption is getting a kind of social acceptability? Practically in fact, it is looking like that only. Despite all laws to prevent corruption and the anticorruption wings ailment of corruption could not be stopped and it survived with increased dimensions. Governments failed. Legal provisions proved to be ineffective. The common Indian man was made ultimate sufferer of it. Now we witness the climax of it in form of 'tussle' between government lokpal and jan lokpal. We do not know who of the two claimants are honest enough in their fight against corruption. Only future will tell. Or else it would also prove to be yet another 'political gimmick' befooling us the people of India.

Merely making of laws would not be the final solution of all the problems. It is said about our country India that it is known for 'maximum' of legislations but 'minimum' of implementations. We need to give a serious thought to this impression. No doubt we make laws with full vigor but when it comes to enforcement our system proves to be a failure in enforcing them in true sense. Laws of the country do not function properly and also the offenders flee punishment even after breaking laws. For all such failures to the extent our 'mechanism' is responsible and 'equally' responsible is our society too. Let us expect that by means of 'churning out' proposed lokpals, a strong lokpal would emerge out of it. There are honest suggestions that whatever laws are made it should be 'tough' and provisions for stringent punishment should be provided for corrupt ones. In modern India the Parliament came out with tough laws T.A.D.A. and P.O.T.A. the problem of terrorism is still there in our country but we have done away with these tough anti-terror laws for no cogent reasons. And what become fate of these laws is not hidden from we the citizen of India. Indian society still lives with under the shadow of terrorism left at mercy of the Almighty.

Under Indian penal statutes, for a serious most offence like murder there is strict most punishment of death sentence. It was held by the Supreme Court of India in Bachan Singh's case that for offence of murder, only in 'rarest of the rare' cases death sentence should be awarded. Where the competent trial court finds a case to be one of 'rarest of the rare' and awards death sentence. Confirmation of death sentence under section 366 of Criminal Procedure Code 1973 is statutory necessity by the concerned High Court. The idea behind such confirmation is that before executing death sentence it needs to be legally scrutinized. When we demand for 'stringent' punishment for corrupt ones then what do we statutorily mean it? What do one understand 'meaning' of stringent punishment under the penal statutes? There cannot be a bigger punishment than death in any sentencing system. Our penal justice system does not provide for as to what do we mean by stricter punishment? Do we mean by that, for instance let deep cuts be made by a sharp blade on the entire body of the persons found involved in corruption? Then rub with 'salt' and 'red chili' throughout the cut marks on the body. Make him lie on ice slabs to freezing point and should be sentenced by torturing him to death. Whether such a kind of 'stringent' punishment would be permissible particularly in existing reformatory penal system? Human rights organizations will 'spring' into action crying as to why the 'poor corrupt' person is being tortured like this kind of stringent punishment? The offence he has been charged with is simply corruption as usual. So no strict punishment could be given bigger than death. And looking to criminal psychology of offenders today they are least bothered of death sentence.

The penal mechanism in existing criminal justice system emphasizes more in reforming criminals rather than to punish them. One can easily conclude that let the corrupt ones keep committing corruption and our penal system would remain 'busy' in looking for ways and means to reform them. Once the Parliament came with a proposal that since the offences like rape against women in society are very cruel and barbarous and despite the fact that there is penal provision under Indian Penal Code for punishing the offence of rape but the number of rape crimes are not reduced. The rapists were not feared of such sentence. It was suggested in the Parliament that for controlling rape crimes and with a view to protect women in society section 376 I.P.C. need to be amended and 'strict' punishment should be provided. The proposal was that offence of rape should be made punishable with death sentence. This proposal of strict punishment for rape could not be moved in the Parliament. You should not be surprised to know this fact that before this amendment could have been moved and passed in the Parliament women organizations themselves came forward and strongly opposed this proposed amendment. The plea made by women organizations was that once this law is made now 'life' of women would be in danger. Now rapists would commit not one but two offences. First they will commit rape of women and thereafter they will murder the women so raped with a view to destroy the evidence after rape. Because once law provides death sentence for rape also while murder is already punishable with death then it will come to the mind of rapist that if death is to be given for rape also then why not to kill the rape victim and remove the evidence forever? The rapist now will commit two offences but he will get punishment for one offence only that too when it is proved beyond all reasonable doubts. Otherwise he will be exonerated with full honors for lack of sufficient evidence.

Thus the humble submission is that by merely making laws and by fear of death sentence crimes cannot be stopped in society. Had this fear of laws been there then serious offence like rape and murder would have been stopped. The famous American criminologist Edwin Sutherland who has been exponent of 'sociological school of criminology' has made it clear through his research study that whatever the crimes take place in society, for all that society itself is responsible. Unless the society changes its mindset no laws would be able to have their proper impact to prevent crimes in society. Today what people are talking about lokpals for stopping corruption Edwin Sutherland had already conducted a comprehensive study on the criminal behavior of corruption? According to him the crime of corruption is committed by people of high social status in course of their 'occupation' by means of abusing their official positions. Such crimes dangerously make hollow the entire socio-economic fabric of society. Sutherland named it as while collar crimes and the people who indulge in corruption as white collar criminals. Such criminals have 'lust' for money and are to the extent 'mad' after money. Sutherland considers that since white collar criminals are so highly placed and influential that the law is not in a position to harm them a bit. If a case is registered even then it is so entangled in the procedural formalities of law that trial of case succumbs to it without any delivery of justice.

Suppose a 'strong' lokpal comes into existence and the Parliament makes a 'tough' law also with an objective to deal with corruption with a 'heavy' hand then the foremost condition would be that society should have to come forward along with law in its 'fight' against corruption. There would be situations that just below the nose of the 'tough' anticorruption law and the lokpals people would keep demanding and accepting bribes People would be ready to keep 'offering' bribes to corrupt people without any objection since they would be having their own 'vested' interests in it. Law will not be in a position to see because it is blind? After all who should have to object? Off course the person who is being forced to give bribe. When the person giving bribe has no objection to it then why the person receiving bribe would object? Finally there would be no objection or complaint before the law. Law needs evidence. On the basis of evidence only the law will proceed further and would be in a position to punish the corrupt by a procedure established by law. In matters of public corruption statement and evidence of the person giving bribe is very significant. And if such person gives a statement before the law that he never gave bribe to the accused then provisions of such 'tough' laws would be blown into air. What the law would be in a position to do? Who is coming forward to help the law and give evidences to get corrupt people punished? Corruption could not be ended in this way. Do not blame the law then? Yes..! O K law could be 'strict' and 'tough' but where is the evidence? People only being members of this society who 'induce' and give 'temptations' for bribing and 'motivate' for corruption in their own vested interests will be instrumental in suffocating such 'tough' laws and the corrupt accused persons move around freely thrashing out the anticorruption laws.

Unless there is a comprehensive change of the mindset and mentality of the people in society merely by means of making tough laws we cannot fight the corruption. Let us not presume it that by a tough anticorruption law people with corrupt mindset are going to be scared of it and stop taking bribes and other unlawful considerations. Under criminal laws imposition of death sentence is considered to be a tough statutory provision. Death sentence has been provided for grievous offences like murder. But questions would arise whether by the fear of hanging to death the offenders have stopped killing people in society? The reply would be in negative. Whether criminals are truly scared of hanging to death? No not. Then do we think that corrupt ones would go scared by a 'tough' law and corruption will be stopped in society? What should be the reply? I feel sorry to submit that this perception of no fear of punishment will prove to be very dangerous and will only damage the Indian social-legal conditions. But still if any honest and collective social initiatives are taken up towards fighting corruption and healthy results are coming out of it then such meaningful efforts should always be welcomed.

It must be a genuine concern of us all that our nation India does not get weaker socio-economically. There should be effective regulatory control over corrupt practices. With a view to achieve this objective the law of the nation and legal system of the country be allowed to perform its function independently. Laws are broken in society, crimes are committed and corruption takes place. For all that our culpable mindset in society is to be blamed. For purpose of eradicating corruption from society unless we come forward as responsible citizens to help the laws of the nation it will not be possible for the legal system to properly function. From where the law would get the needed evidence to punish offenders? We need to stop finding faults with our legal system just in our desperate bid to conceal our own worthlessness. If we continued to think like that only corruption will keep happening and the nation would be unable to come out of the peril of socio-economic injustice. Our nation will get hollow, weak and weak. We would have to come forward to save our nation or who will else? We need a socio-economically strong nation to be on top of the world. We have the potential now what we require is change of our mindset pragmatically.

"Unless the society changes its mindset no laws would be able to have their proper impact to prevent crimes in society. Today what people are talking about lokpals for stopping corruption Edwin Sutherland had already conducted a comprehensive study on the criminal behavior of corruption? According to him the crime of corruption is committed by people of high social status in course of their 'occupation' by means of abusing their official positions. Such crimes dangerously make hollow the entire socio-economic fabric of society."

84

Police Reforms- Bare Truths

Police system is most significant pillar of criminal justice administration. Policing is essential for an orderly society and maintenance of law and order. Police system has not only to ensure prevention of crime but also in case of happening of crimes police has to perform the task of investigation. By means of conducting investigation of criminal cases police exercises statutory powers given under law to collect evidences so that get the criminals punished on the basis of evidences so collected during the course of investigation.

Looking back to establishment of police system in India it goes back to the Police Act 1861 which even today controls and regulates the Indian police machinery. The Police Act 1861 was passed in British Parliament and was enforced in India during the British rule. Technically this Act more appears to be a British Charter to rule India according to their own calculations rather than to serve any public interest including the police. During the year 1861 circumstances were completely different when the Britain introduced this Act in India completely with a ruler's mind set. This Act puts more emphasis on enforcement of orders of the superior officers and the government directives rather than for protection of the rights of the public. After we got independence from British we adopted the Police Act 1861 as such.

We forgot this fact that now after its adoption in totality the Act would be in force in democratically independent India rather than the India under British rule. We also forgot that its enforcement in free India as such would reflect the British mindset in day to day functioning of our police and it would in long turn jeopardize police-public relations adversely affecting the Indian social fabric. We witness on regular basis strained police-public relationship. Did we ever think about the reasons behind? Can any police system function justifiably without active and honest cooperation of the public? Certainly not. Strained police-public relations give rise to social ill will followed by social disorder. One feels very sorry to see that in India most hated government official in the eyes of public are the police constables. Same treatment they come across in their departments at the hands of their higher ups.

Police officers are twenty four hours on duty. They are blamed for indulging in corruption, keeping nexus with criminals that's why failing in crime prevention. Their role is questioned during communal violence. Cases of custodial violence and rape are also not uncommon. May be some of allegations against them appear to be true. But could we sincerely think about the reasons behind it? Do we remember our policemen who were killed protecting Parliament House? They sacrifice their life fighting criminals, naxalites and terrorists. While patrolling in society their life is not safe. This is because of reasons that the criminal gangs are better equipped with weapons when compared to our police force. While on duty the policemen have to live far away from their family member for a considerable span of time. More than 80 percent of police force under any state government comprises of police constables and they are solely accountable for maintenance of law and order and internal security of the nation. Conditions of such policemen are very painful. They are the most exploited lot in the name of discipline. They are not well paid salary wise and their promotions avenues in the department are also not much encouraging. A good number of our policemen work as domestic help to their superior officers. This is not their part of duty but they are not able to refuse for the reasons of disciplinary action on one pretext or the other. What the kind of law enforcement do we expect from them under such unhealthy prevailing situations?

On front of police reforms the system came out with Police Commissions, Gore Committee, Ribero Committee etc. Despite notable recommendations by these commissions on fronts of police reforms nothing concrete could come out to boost the morale of police personnel. Not only we require psychological conditions of our policemen to be improved but they also need to be well equipped with modern weapons to deal with criminals face to face. Politicization of police is also proving to be very critical since under such situations one cannot expect the police personnel to act neutral above political considerations. Is it possible in a political feel set up like India? This is a question which needs a deep introspection by caretakers of system. Unless the system makes our police force feel psychologically secure and strong it appears to be practically difficult to make the system upright. Police are force of 'state' and they should be allowed to work above political calculations then only they would be in a position to infuse a kind of trust with public. Policemen are also human beings after all and not the machines. What the most needed for them is positive reforms in their service conditions with a humane touch of social respect.

"We also forgot that its enforcement in free India as such would reflect the British mindset in day to day functioning of our police and it would in long turn jeopardize police-public relations adversely affecting the Indian social fabric. We witness on regular basis strained police-public relationship. Did we ever think about the reasons behind?"

85

Judicial Activism and Beyond

Judiciary is always active. Judicial activism should not be understood in terms that judiciary is 'seen active' only on selective occasions. Active judiciary gets adversely affected by manipulative tactics of litigants to delay the proceeding one way or the other. Due to manipulation of legal procedure the court proceedings are so prolonged for an uncertain period that even if justice is 'delivered' at last but it is so 'delayed' that now it is of no use. Judicial authorities cannot claim that it remained completely 'innocent' throughout about the manipulative motives of the litigants. Judiciary also cannot claim that the things went absolutely out of its control to set the things right. Justice delayed has become so 'proverbial' to the extent that it communicates it all regarding existing state of affairs in Indian Judiciary. Judicial action needs to be seen in fast disposal of cases and delivery of judgments at least if could not go for delivery of justice.

Judicial activism came to be established as a phenomenon in Indian judicial and justice delivery system. Legal fraternity would never forget great contributions of Justice P.N. Bhagwati, Justice Krishna Iyer and Justice Rangnath Mishra who 'dared' to go beyond the established practice of legal procedure for the sake of ensuring delivery of justice to the people at large. These revolutionary judges made it known to the judicial world that the 'rule of locus standi' would have to go if it creates hindrances in the pious task of administration justice to common men in public interest. Now it was for the next generations in line to follow so that justice should 'appear' to have been done. But you just cannot help. It takes generations for such judicial brains to born who make history to be imprinted in golden letters once for all.

Judicial activism could be literally defined as where the judiciary goes active extra ordinarily breaking procedural 'barriers' and vigilantly taking stock of the situations particularly where there appears to be colorable exercise of administrative authority. Not only that but where there are reports of administrative inaction the judiciary takes cognizance of it 'suo motu' because under existing circumstances of inaction the justice administration is of the opinion that if the circumstances are allowed to continue further it would jeopardize legal interests of many. Such a situation should not be allowed to happen since it would amount to be a great injustice to the people whose legal rights are violated and not enforced largely due to administrative inaction.

And also for the reasons that every citizen in India is financially not capable enough to seek legal protection from judiciary. Legal advice has become very expensive these days so people economically weak would not be able to seek remedy from the court of law and their legal rights would continue to be violated. Judicial activism could be a guiding principle for next generation judicial officers but in deeper sense this is only a state of mind of an individual judge with a bit of 'determination' for the sake of justice delivery. Once he decides that justice is to be administered he is unstoppable. The sensible mind of the judge which goes 'restless' when it hears of violation of legal rights of people and when it finds itself 'entangled' with procedural 'bottlenecks' of the justice system. And that too when it notices that the administrative set up takes undue advantage of such bottlenecks in denying justice to the public. When a sensible judicial brain goes restless of the existing state of affairs it 'cries out' with what is termed as judicial activism.

Judicial passiveness goes in contra distinction to judicial activism. Judicial passiveness is not uncommon basically for the scientific reasons that every judicial mind is not supposed to be a genius one. But honest efforts could be made at least for the sake of just and fair administration of justice to all. A laborious mind can quite significantly convert it into as equal to a genius one. Judicial activism should be applied very judiciously so that it does not appear to be amounting to interfering with the process of law. On occasions the apex court has warned against excessive judicial activism. Does it hint at someway abuse of the legal process by higher judiciary? If it is then it will prove to be detrimental to the law and justice. Let us not allow the situations so happen and to be ready with preventive steps to avoid maligning of the image of active judiciary by referring it to as judicial terrorism. If they succeeded in their design to discourage the great phenomenon of judicial activism then justice will not reach to the 'people' who are truly in need of justice. Let us remember that under such circumstances only the 'justice' would be the ultimate looser. The justice be saved from being lost. This the judicial activism can only do.

"The sensible mind of the judge which goes 'restless' when it hears of violation of legal rights of people and when it finds itself 'entangled' with procedural 'bottlenecks' of the justice system. And that too when it notices that the administrative set up takes undue advantage of such bottlenecks in denying justice to the public. When a sensible judicial brain goes restless of the existing state of affairs it 'cries out' with what is termed as judicial activism."

86

Do Not Play With Environment

We can understand global concerns for protection of our environment. A complete environmental jurisprudence has been developed all across the world to address the environment related issues. Global march could only be ensured with 'march' of environment. Environment has its own rules and regulations to control with. Environment has its own steps to march with. Rules of environment are well knit with to ensure a definite balance in environmental system. With passage of time as the evidences reveal it is the human agency only which plays destructive role with balancing mechanism of environment. If human agency is out to 'disturb' the 'natural balancing' of environment then it is hereby warned that human agencies should keep ready for an imbalanced environment. Survival of mankind on this earth is directly proportional to a healthy environment. Not only mankind but survival of flora and fauna is also equally essential for maintaining the natural 'ecological balance'.

The big challenge now-a-days before us is the protection of environment from pollution and from destruction of its natural resources. Due to fast and 'unplanned' modernization, the environment had to pay adversely. Environmental resources have their own natural limitations whereas our developmental 'ambitions' are getting unlimited. Developmental ambitions are good but not at cost of destroying environment. To facilitate fast growing 'concrete jungles' we have mercilessly cut down our wooden jungles. Natural environmental cycles are broken. Poisonous gases are out in atmosphere due to heavy transportation on the roads and rapid industrialization. People living in metros and other big cities are struggling tough for fresh air in the atmosphere to breath in. The environmental scientists are able to pin point the factors behind depletion of ozone layer from atmosphere and they have also warned about its future consequences.

But it appears that modern civilizations are not taking serious note of it. Otherwise how come it would have been possible that the 'global warming' so close to us has already started knocking to at our door steps? How long civilizations would keep mum and would not respond to such knocking signals from the nature? Make it a point my friends..! That you cannot control and regulate the environment by means of your statutory provisions whether national or international. If 'tsunami' has to come, it has to come. You just cannot stop it. What you just can do only is to release precautionary signals minimize your loss? That's all. Fortunately those who are equipped with to catch your precautionary signals well within time they would be able to vacate going to be affected areas and manage to save their life. Otherwise those who are not able to get these precautions they would be 'buried' with aftermath of devastating scenario. The world has been helplessly a mute spectator to such environmental devastations in past only to start rehabilitation with whatever is left behind and pray the Almighty for a safer world.

The Almighty would definitely listen to our prayers provided we are prepared to listen to the 'calls' of our environment. If we turn a careless blind ear to the calls of our environment for protecting and preserving it then friends sorry..! Almighty is not going to listen to our prayers. We should keep ready to face 'consequences' of our unnatural deeds. Playing with the environment is quite unnatural. Recent devastating environmental tragedy of Uttarakhand in India which took thousands of people's life should be an eye opener not only to the environmental managers but also to the people at large. People at large also play a contributory role in 'teasing' with the environment.

When observed minutely then we would see that we have started experiencing 'minor shifts' in commencement of the major seasons round the year. Extreme 'cooling' conditions in winter and equally extreme 'warm' conditions in summers now getting natural order and is something very strange for environmental scientists. The environment scientists perceive this 'shifting' to be an indication for a major 'environmental upheaval' in future years. This would be definitely damaging for the mankind if we do not stop playing with the environment. Statutory provisions would not help anyway unless the people themselves come out with firm determinations that the environment has to be protected at any cost. Let us do 'justice' with the environment at least for our own sake then only we can think about environment doing 'justice' to us.

"The Almighty would definitely listen to our prayers provided we are prepared to listen to the 'calls' of our environment. If we turn a careless blind ear to the calls of our environment for protecting and preserving it then friends sorry..! Almighty is not going to listen to our prayers. We should keep ready to face 'consequences' of our unnatural deeds. Playing with the environment is quite unnatural."

87

Let Justice Appear To Be Done?

In the system of justice administration there is a very famous saying that 'justice should not only be done but it should also appear to have been done'. It is very 'easy' to define term justice. No educational qualification is needed for a man to do justice. Justice simply means as to what is just, fair and reasonable in given situations and circumstances. What is rightfully to be done? And what has not been prohibited by law? In layman's perception even justice is quite 'communicative' and 'understandable' provided we see to it through their perceptions. Affording opportunity to be heard is a natural parameter of justice administration. An 'alert' mind which is absolutely 'unbiased' with its eyes 'shut' and ears 'open' would be the fountain of justice that's the condition. Do we fulfill these conditions? Query could be made as to how long one would be in a position to keep his eyes 'shut'? It is a very tough task but that is the condition of law. Another big question people may raise that as to how one would be able to ensure a 'consistently alert mind' that too with an absolute 'unbiasness'?

A simple reply to this big question is that such people are very 'rare' with consistently alert mind. The conclusion would also be the fact then that justice is also very rare. Otherwise it would not have been 'proverbial' that justice should not only be 'done' but it should 'appear' to have been done to the people at large. People with an unbiased mind in society do scale up the judgments so delivered by the courts. They do not understand the 'procedural complicacies' what the courts have to unfold throughout the trial of the cases before it. What they feel is that there is no need to understand about the procedural complicacies? They see the judgment only being final outcome of the entire rigorous legal process prolonging across decades. Yes..!!! only to know that there is no justice done albeit the judgment has been finally delivered.

The burning question of the day is that why to make the justice suffer through the procedural complicacies of law only to know after decades of hearings that though judgment has been given finally but justice could not be delivered? Can't we make the procedure as simple as that the justice delivery itself? It is for aforesaid reasons only that it is becoming highly proverbial these days that 'judgments would be only delivered in courts but not the justice'. No one can deny that procedural complexities give 'room' for 'manipulative' tactics to the litigants. Honestly speaking such manipulations are not unknown to the managers of Indian legal system. How courts can claim to be completely ignorant about it? When manipulations 'creep' in the system that too in full knowledge of system, one can imagine as to how it would become practically difficult for the system to 'remove' those manipulations which are by now 'set in' the system? Once manipulations set in with system it could be any body's guess the layman including that now judgments only would be delivered. Forget about justice. The system comes out with a very heavy heart to deliver the 'justice' in the form of delivery of its judgment only to impress upon that the 'justice' so delivered under the prevailing circumstance will never 'appear' to be. The justice now becomes part of the court records only to rest in peace. The procedure after wards to follow for the litigants takes them up to the appellate courts. Still at least two stages of appeal are to welcome the justice which is yet to be 'finally' delivered. For lot many litigants it proves to be a never ending process in the meantime they depart for their heavenly abode. And the final justice lays with the Almighty that's yet another proverb that one get justice in heavens only. Who knows? None came back from heavens to say it only that they got 'justice' finally.

It's high time for caretakers of system to give a serious thought to existing justice delivery system so as to ensure the 'justice' appearing to be. Not that judgment only is delivered. This fact is not to be denied that we are the justice system completely banking upon borrowed system from British. They used to make law for us in British Parliament and then 'enforce' upon us so as to facilitate and 'tighten' grips of their rule over India. It goes without saying that their legal mechanism applied in India was for protecting the interests of the rulers and not the ruled ones. We adopted all that afterwards without much hesitation. British introduced procedural legal complications in India so that they can rule over India without much opposition. And keep the 'ruled ones busy' in fighting out legal complications. If England can deliver constitutional justice to its citizen without any written Constitution in their country then why does the 'borrowed procedural complications' for India? We can endeavor to do justice which would also appear to be to the common man's perceptions. We need our own 'indigenous' legal system to deliver with justice by keeping principles of natural justice intact.

> *"It goes without saying that their legal mechanism applied in India was for protecting the interests of the rulers and not the ruled ones. We adopted all that afterwards without much hesitation. British introduced procedural legal complications in India so that they can rule over India without much opposition. And keep the 'ruled ones busy' in fighting out legal complications."*

88

Agricultural Economy

Agricultural economy we mean where majority of population in India adopts agriculture based occupations for earning their livelihood. India is an Agriculture major country. I am not in a position to define economics from viewpoint of an economist but in simple layman's language this thing one needs to compulsorily understand that where every person in the society could be in a position to earn at least an income for his livelihood as his purchase capacity to fulfillment his day to day minimum requirements. Also at the same time he is able to keep some money for making his essential saving out of such earnings. Out of his small savings he could be able to fulfill his future and other emergent requirements.

According to official data in India about 70 to 75 percent population is completely dependent for its income either on agriculture or agriculture base occupations. Out of this 70 to 75 percent population all are not similar. All do not possess agricultural land on which they could grow crops and could sell agricultural products for their earnings. There are classes of people who are landless and work on other's land as labor for their survival. Had situations of agricultural economy been there and also dependable one then nothing could have been better than that. And merely based upon 'agricultural economy' only the farmers of Indian nation would have been seen prosperous. We did make laws relating to abolition of 'zamindari system' but we failed their honest enforcement. We could not provide agricultural land to landless classes of people according to their requirement so that they could survive on their hard work. The very objective behind zamindari abolition was that the land lords who are in their possession a disproportionate quantity of agricultural land i.e. more than their requirements, ceiling should be imposed on them and extra land be given in the name of needy landless class. Could we do that? If we could not do that then the advantage of agricultural based economy remained limited among 'handful' of zamindars and the landless even today remained as labor only on the fields of these zamindars and were subject to exploitation.

We talk about our growing prosperity in the fields of agricultural products which were land based and our self dependence. We also find ourselves in a position to export agriproducts to different nations but in our own country we fail to fulfill food requirements of majority class of people who have no land resources with them to work and grow. Agricultural productivity largely depends upon 'mood' of the nature. Untimely rains or famines destroy agricultural productivity. At the same time heavy rains destroys fully grown crops. Winter acute chilly cold conditions completely ruin crops. There is no adequate system management in flood hit areas. Even in the modern technologically advanced world we are yet not able to search for effective means to prevent floods so as to permanently get rid of flood disasters. The stages of nature are beyond the control of agricultural mechanism it is not like that. We are 'heard' talking about 'prompt' disaster management by that time heavy damage is already done to crops and the farmer had to suffer irreparable loss. After disaster stabilizes our entire disaster management comes in a relax mode as if now waiting for the next disaster. But still if our 'waiting' appears to be alert then things could have been controlled considerably and possibly we would be in a position to deal with disasters effectively. But when our 'management' begins by that time the 'disaster' goes after causing huge destruction.

In the shadow of these natural uncertainties and calamities perhaps big farmers would be in a position to get back their invested sum but the small and medium farmers are heard crying out even losing their initial investment in the profession of agriculture. Farmers committing suicide under such circumstances are not unheard of in India. It should not be a matter of surprise that due to uncertainty in profits and for fears of losing their initial investments even the farmers are getting 'detached' from agriculture. As a result we witness growing urbanization in search of employment.

Presence of active 'mediators' in agricultural economics is major factor to failing agricultural management system. The government purchase centers of agriproducts remain 'not so active' whereas the mediators are seen 'much active'. Small and medium farmers do not have any means to take their grains and other products to government purchase centers. Whereas the brokers give them this facility at their doorsteps. One is unable to understand whether the government system is better equipped or else these brokers? But the truth is just opposite to it. The crux of agricultural economics is that a greater portion of hard earned money of farmers is 'eaten' away by these brokers who have nothing to do with the work of agriculture. This is very unfair situation and beyond comprehension. It is not like that our agriculture management system is completely unaware about active presence of these brokers in agricultural markets but for reasons of its own vested interests in brokers the system turns a 'blind eye'. The system getting absolutely helpless in handling these brokers goes against economic interests of the farmers. It's quite natural that farmers should get reasonable cost of their labor. Existence of parallel systems of mediators is not a good indication for government management. Under these situations only 'mismanagement' makes its inroads in the system and generates opportunities for injustice to the farmers.

> *"The crux of agricultural economics is that a greater portion of hard earned money of farmers is 'eaten' away by these brokers who have nothing to do with the work of agriculture. This is very unfair situation and beyond comprehension. It is not like that our agriculture management system is completely unaware about active presence of these brokers in agricultural markets but for reasons of its own vested interests in brokers the system turns a 'blind eye'."*

89

Sociology of Crimes

It is the society 'itself' which is responsible for criminal behavior in a person. There are well defined sociological characteristics prevalent in societies which generate crimes. Criminal behavior is learnt in society itself. Famous American criminologist Edwin Sutherland came out with his research findings that for understanding criminal behavior in a person we need not to go elsewhere but if we search for the factors in and around then we would find that crimogenic factors are already present within society. According to Sutherland it is due to 'differential association' with 'criminally intimate groups' that a person learns criminal behavior by imitating these criminally intimate groups. The persons who have criminal tendency come easily in close association with criminal groups. A person does not develop criminal tendency by birth. He falls victim of certain social situations and circumstances which are not within his control and commits crime. Such criminals are termed as situational or occasional criminals. They should not be blamed for prevalence of crimogenic situation in society. It is for caretakers of social systems to ensure that crimogenic situations do not set in. If it does then people with criminal tendency do not remain unaffected by it. Crimogenic situations in society relate to such situations which generate crimes. It would always remain a point of relevance that if society endeavors to minimize crimogenic situations from the society then we would be in a position to reduce crime rates happening in society. It is obvious conclusion that had the crimogenic situations not been there in society then crime would not have taken place. Because it was existence of crimogenic situation only which compelled the person to commit crime.

Lack of proper education is the most important causative factor which could be attributed to increasing trends in criminal behavior. Providing proper education to its people is a crucial social responsibility. A person who has been properly educated by society would find positive reflection of such education in his day to day personal behavior. Criminal behavior in a person reflects 'negative orientation' of mindset of the person. A person orients negatively because of lack of proper education. He does not find himself logically in a position to distinguish between what is good to him and what is bad for him to do? Had he been properly educated he would have definitely thought once that he should not do crimes. Once criminal tendency dominates over the person his logical thinking mind goes to the back seat. Due to lack of education his lesser logical mind fails to counter his criminal mind and he commits crimes. Criminality has a kind of temptation to break criminal laws because it exhibits a show of strength among other members of society. Show of power domination tempts them to be habitual and repeaters of crimes.

Even proper education does not help in reducing unemployment. Large scale unemployment among youth has proved to be a significant crimogenic factor what the researches have revealed. It has been found that when there was regular increasing rate of unemployment there was increase in rate of crimes also as recorded at police stations. Therefore the finding is that a direct proportional relationship has been noticed between increasing rate of unemployment and increasing rate of crime. This relationship clearly establishes that if societies are able to generate adequate employment opportunities for unemployed youth they will remain busy with their employment, think constructively and they would not involve themselves in criminal activities. It has also been found that professional criminal groups very easily attract such unemployed youth towards crimes because they are paid for criminal act by these professionals.

Where social system fails in generating adequate employment opportunities owing to which a big number of youth are attracted toward economic offences so as to fulfill their economic necessities. Therefore society should keep ready to face consequences of not properly educating their youth and also in failing to get them proper employment. Now the big question is whether to what extent such youth are responsible for their criminal behavior where society fails to arrange for them proper work to do? Such youth who are sensitive enough easily come in contacts with criminal groups. No need to say that they are attracted by glamour of the crime world. Criminals have their own world to enjoy. It proves to be a failure on part of the social system managers that they let sociology of crime flourish that's why in social circles categories of crimes are adopted as profession. It also confers a kind of social status for criminals in the eyes of members of society. Once the criminal gangs establish a nexus with law enforcements than sociology of crimes for them becomes much easier and our deviated youth decide to stay in criminal world for ever and goes with an alarming signal to society.

"Where social system fails in generating adequate employment opportunities owing to which a big number of youth are attracted toward economic offences so as to fulfill their economic necessities. Therefore society should keep ready to face consequences of not properly educating their youth and also in failing to get them proper employment. Now the big question is whether to what extent such youth are responsible for their criminal behavior where society fails to arrange for them proper work to do?"

90

Consumers of Adulterated Food

S elling of adulterated food in markets without any sense of fear has become common practice. The matter of worry is that people have no 'choice' except knowing it fully well that they are 'consuming adulterated food' and moving closer to death. Under the compulsions of situations people go philosophical and are heard saying one day or the other they have to die after all. They are not born to be immortal. What is the other way out? Such sellers of spoiled food have no terror of law either in their mind and system also lies inactive. One wonders to see all that and is painful too.

Adulterated food is that of which 'quality' and 'nutritional value' is adversely destroyed due to adulteration. It is done by the manufactures and sellers of food articles in an unlawful manner with a dishonest intention to earn wrongful gain. In the name of selling particular food item the seller would charge full market price of the item from the consumer. But due to impurities in it the quality of the food article would be lower and it would be even harmful for the health of the consumer. There is a very strange law in statute books 'buyer be aware'. As if the buyer only has to be careful where the sellers are licensed and made free to sell anything in the market. Now it is the headache of buyer only to take care while purchasing articles from the market. Do we mean by it that while going to market for purchase the buyer is expected to carry all 'measurements with him' for quality check? On every step he should test and examine quality of goods satisfy him and then only buy it. Otherwise he will be made to understand that 'things once sold shall not be returned'. How many of such buyers would be there in markets that possess expertise to examine quality of adulterated food articles? Our food inspectors also collect specimen of such adulterated food and send it to food laboratory for its chemical analysis to test percentage of impurities and its quality. Burden of taking care lies on buyer only. Such principle of law is not understandable. Making efforts to understand means unnecessary wastage of time and useless mental exercise. The thing which one is able to understand easily is that if the consumer failed in taking care then let him suffer. Should not burden the system unnecessarily. System had already cautioned him.

In the modern new era people are dying of very strange kind of physical and mental diseases. Medical science also remains almost ignorant of such diseases. Doctors too give treatment as per symptoms and are not able to reach to the root cause and the patient dies. When adulteration is all around may be somewhere less or somewhere more, the consumers have only two choices before him. He has to choose either of the two. He is helpless. Meaning thereby he has to 'purchase' adulteration for a price. Even nature borne fruits and vegetables are also not safe from adulteration. Whatever is available in markets the consumer has to purchase that and consume it, no way? Adulterated foods have given rise to newer kinds of physical and mental diseases to consumers. Now-a-days you would have definitely noticed 'never ending big rush' on medicine shops from morning till evening. People are destined to die but the rush on medicine shops keeps growing. Never wonder..! Spurious drugs are also available in huge quantity on medicine shops. Where would you go? What are the choices before you? Either your life or else death. The conclusion comes out to be that the consumers would not be in a position to get rid of adulteration right from their life to death. And nobody is in a position to make any such claim that he is not a consumer therefore he is safe.

Situations of selling of adulterated food are getting highly fearsome and most of injustice too. You will buy your slow death from market by paying price of it. Food adulteration is like a slow poison. The poison of impurities would leave their impact on your mind and body slowly and slowly. By consuming adulterated food you will not die all of sudden but due to impurities your body would become victim of diseases internally. Nervous cells of your mind would go weak and weak. Your body would have life but your body would not be healthy. Your mind would be reflecting movements but you will not feel to be mentally alert and strong. The doctor will provide all treatment to your disease but he will not be in a position to help you out from selling of adulterated food in consumer markets. He cannot help to stop it. Who knows that you develop some other 'ailment' due to impurities and adulteration? The doctor was attending to your treatment in the meantime you complained about some new problem. Today it is becoming a very common thing. Very serious and worry some changes are being noticed. The changes are very dangerous for human health. Doctors are bound to advise that a particular treatment would go life long, a particular medicine one need to take whole life. In recent years percentage of people's dependency on medicines has increased very fast. May be we claim this as well that average life span of people has also increased. Undoubtedly, it could become possible only due to sustained research in the field of medical sciences. But as far as question of human health is concerned much dependency in life on medicines is not a healthy signal.

Under legal systems selling of adulterated food has been kept in the category of strict criminal liability. Where criminal intention of the seller for doing this crime is not needed to be proved. Sorry states of affair are that adulterated food are openly sold and have made a strong control over the market system just below the nose of food inspectors. Our administrative and legal institutions appear to be quite weak. We need to come forward with a collective effort and look for solid reasons and search such measures so that the consumer gets quality for a price and not slow poison. It must be taken as warning that under aforementioned circumstances our society would continue to be diseased, hollow and weak. We have to save our nation from becoming weak and do justice for the nation.

"How many of such buyers would be there in markets that possess expertise to examine quality of adulterated food articles? Our food inspectors also collect specimen of such adulterated food and send it to food laboratory for its chemical analysis to test percentage of impurities and its quality. Burden of taking care lies on buyer only. Such principle of law is not understandable."

91

Deterrence of Punishment

Punishment is the only method under criminal justice system to deter criminals. Various theories of punishment finally conclude that punishment should be imposed upon criminals otherwise it would be very difficult to control crimes in society. There are no two opinions about it but the purpose behind imposing such punishment may vary in crime to the other looking to gravity of crimes. By means of imposing punishment creating a kind of fear of it in the mind of the criminals is the main objective behind punishment. Not only for criminals but for the people at large it serves a kind of deterrent message and which has a preventive effect on criminal behavior of people. If we examine different modes of punishment permitted under statute books we find impact of deterrent theory of punishment. Theoretical aspects of punishment find its representation one way or the other. But it becomes a matter of serious concern for the administrators of criminal justice when it is noticed that despite all punishments it fails to have its preventive effect. Criminal activities go unabated and system fails to stop crimes in society. Increasing crime rate and the undeterred 'modus operandi' of criminals is an indicator to the fact that punishments cease to have its 'fear impact' on criminals.

The question of worry for the system should be as to what would amount to 'deter' criminals from committing crimes? What will happen to the situations of law and order once the fear of punishment is gone out of the mind of criminals? The system cannot impose a kind of punishment on criminals other than what is prescribed in penal statutes. And if the lawful 'modes of punishment' provided under penal statutes fail to achieve its objectives then what would the alternative left behind for the administrators of criminal justice system to deal with criminals under these circumstances? What do we mean by the deterrence of punishment? Under criminal penal jurisprudence the nature of punishment is basically 'corporal' in nature. The quantum of punishment increases with increasing gravity of crime committed by a particular criminal. Whether the deterrence of punishment is more psychological or more physical?

Penal statutes do not permit for physical torture of a convict. He has to just undergo the 'span of imprisonment' behind the bars as imposed by the courts with all human rights admissible to prisoners intact. If he is to be hanged finally that too only in 'rarest of the rare' situations then it should be with strict observance to basics of human rights jurisprudence. The worries relating to observance of basic tenets of human rights are absolutely undisputed. One should be in full agreement with the principle is that every criminal too has basic human rights to be protected within the ambit of laws. We forget at the same time that victim of crime too had basic human rights which were brutally thrashed at the hands of criminals. Where the system remained silent spectator to all that. It could only reach at the spot by that time perpetrators of crime had already left the scene. The agencies of law enforcement were helplessly left with only option to 'manage last rites' of the victim as early as possible. For the reasons best known to the system only. This question always remains 'unanswered' whether to what extent the system is 'sensitive' towards human rights of the victims of crimes as well? There are big numbers of human rights organizations also which advocate for protection of and promotion of human rights of convicts. True the convicts too have basic human rights to protect with. But situations go worse when human rights organizations question very legality of punishment to the convicts as awarded by legal system of the country. This tendency virtually defeats aims and objects behind punishment and it gets open to all kind of abuse.

A close study of mind of the criminals would reveal that deterrence of punishment should be more 'psychological' rather 'physical'. Unless it makes an impact on their mind deterrence of punishment would fail. Protracted legal trials in the courts of law are most significant factors behind diminishing deterrence of punishment from mind of criminals. Prolonged trials give them a feel that now their counsel would be able to get them out of the clutches of law. Once out of the clutches of law deterrence of punishment goes away from the mind of the criminal forever. Now it becomes comparatively easier for him to repeat the crime only to become professional. We need to 'fast track' the criminals through speedy trials only then they will fear punishment and deter to commit crime.

"We forget at the same time that victim of crime too had basic human rights which were brutally thrashed at the hands of criminals. Where the system remained silent spectator to all that. It could only reach at the spot by that time perpetrators of crime had already left the scene. The agencies of law enforcement were helplessly left with only option to 'manage last rites' of the victim as early as possible. For the reasons best known to the system only."

92

Fair Trial and Speedy Justice

Trial procedure has been prescribed under the law for conducting trial of cases by a competent court having jurisdiction. In trial of criminal cases basically, the law on procedure has been very significant from legality point of view. Trial could be defined as the procedure to be followed by the trial courts to provide opportunity of hearing to either of the parties in any matter before courts. In criminal cases the prosecution side will be given opportunity to bring evidence in support of the charges leveled by it against the accused person so as to prove that the particular 'fact' existed. Existence of a fact from the prosecution side means that there are evidences to show that the accused committed crime. While the opportunity is to be given to the accused person to produce evidences in his defense to show that the charges so leveled by prosecution side did not exist. This means from the defense side that the evidences produced by the prosecution are without basis and that there are evidence to show that the accused did not commit crime and that he is innocent.

Fair trial means it is responsibility of the trial courts to ensure that the trial process so conducted was absolutely just and fair. The trial procedure has been followed strictly in accordance with law. 'Right to life' and 'right to personal liberty' is most important fundamental right under any criminal jurisprudence of the world. During trials in criminal matters if the accused person has been proved 'guilty' then he would be convicted with corporal punishment either in the form of death sentence or punishment of imprisonment depending upon gravity of the crime. Fundamental right to life and personal liberty makes it expressly clear that 'no person shall be deprived of his life and personal liberty except by a procedure established by law'. Therefore, if an accused person has been convicted either with death sentence or imprisonment then he is going to be deprived from his life or personal liberty as the case may be. Principles of criminal jurisprudence and the constitutional parameters make a categorical declaration that this can only be done by a 'procedure' established by law.

Before imposing any kind of physical punishment on the accused person it is for the trial court to satisfy itself that trial of the case has been conducted in absolute fairness of the procedure, in a transparent manner and by affording adequate opportunity of hearing to both the parties concerned. At the time of commencement of trial the court is not supposed to proceed with unless and until the court is prima facie satisfied about the fact that case is made out. Those too in serious matters the courts are not supposed to go by merely on the basis of charge sheet filed by the police-prosecution side. The courts are required under law to frame charges on its own. When it appears to the trial court that looking to the facts and circumstances in the charge sheet, evidences adduced and after listening to the prosecution and the accused if it prima facie appears to the court that charges are made out the court would proceed with framing of charges. Otherwise the court will 'discharge' the accused person without commencing with the trial for the reasons of lack of proper evidence.

In all fairness of trials the intention of law is that right in the beginning of trial itself it must be 'seen' that the accused should not be put to unnecessary harassment and rigors of the prolonged trial. While the trial court frames the charges against the accused person. The court is duty bound not only to 'read' out the charges to the accused but also to 'explain' the charges to the accused so that in all fairness and to satisfaction of the court the accused is able to properly understand the nature of the charges against him so that he is able to defend himself fairly. Discharge proceedings are for 'speedy justice' so is the 'speedy trial' before memory of the witness starts fading away. 'Justness' and 'fairness' of trial lay in the fact that no innocent person should be put to face unnecessary trial proceedings. This is a very tough judicial function to pin point right at the commencement of the trial itself to 'decide' that if the accused deserves to be discharged? There is a distinction between 'discharge' and 'acquittal' of the accused. In case of acquittal the case has been decided on 'merits' finally while in 'discharge' police can 'reinvestigate' collect further evidence and go for fresh trial. But once the accused person has been acquitted by the competent court the police cannot reinvestigate and prosecute the accused again.

"Discharge proceedings are for 'speedy justice' so is the 'speedy trial' before memory of the witness starts fading away. 'Justness' and 'fairness' of trial lay in the fact that no innocent person should be put to face unnecessary trial proceedings. This is a very tough judicial function to pin point right at the commencement of the trial itself to 'decide' that if the accused deserves to be discharged? There is a distinction between 'discharge' and 'acquittal' of the accused. In case of acquittal the case has been decided on 'merits' finally while in 'discharge' police can 'reinvestigate' collect further evidence and go for fresh trial. But once the accused person has been acquitted by the competent court the police cannot reinvestigate and prosecute the accused again."

93

Ethics goes Professional

The distinction between 'professional ethics' and the 'ethics getting professional' needs to be understood. Every profession has its own code of conduct and it is not only demand of morality but also of law that particular persons should follow the code of conduct of their profession. Following of code of conduct should not be seen by linking it from morality of law. This question is raised very often whether code of conduct comes within the ambit of moral liability only or it has some statutory liability also? A person should have a particular kind of conduct such is his moral liability. If the person does not bring his particular conduct into his behavior then whether within the parameters of law he can be forced to behave such conduct? Whether 'morality of conduct' is enforceable under the law? Under the principles of law this fact finds mention that morality cannot be enforced by law. The logic given is that may be a particular conduct in a given society is collectively acceptable but the same conduct in another society is understood to be objectionable. Then should we leave the morality of a particular conduct on judicious discretion of the person only? Judicious discretions are also to be taken into account when enforceability of conduct is to be ensured under the law. For instance may be the 'live in' relationships between men and women do not stand up to the moral standards of social conduct society considers such relationships to be immoral but our legal institutions decline to interfere with such socially immoral conducts.

There is a difference between 'individual ethics' and 'professional ethics'. Individual conduct if objectionable would be limited to few people only and would not harm society at large but objectionable professional conduct would be harmful to entire society and would adversely affect social interests. Where it would reveal that circumstances are like entire social interests are not safe enforceability of law would have to come forward in greater interest of society. In our society there are number of such professions where role of professional conduct is very significant and sensitive too. Sensitive in the sense that such a professional conduct is directly linked with the trust of people in society. The people have such a trust on the professional men that it never comes to mind of people that he would do such a serious violation of his professional conduct. There is an interesting psychological difference in persons 'being professional' and the persons 'going professional'. Being professional is not bad. Person will work hard honestly and charge full price of it without hesitation. After all what is wrong in it? There are several such professional who do not compromise with the price of their hard work. They always maintain a definite distance between their profession and social personal relationships and liabilities there upon. They never allow to 'mixing up' their profession with social personal responsibilities. Their professional attitude is understandable and nobody should have any objection to it. But difficulty arises and that too it becomes objectionable when their 'professional ethics goes on getting professional'. Ethics getting professional means now the limits of humanity would also be thrashed out. The price of 'labor' would be fully charged with to an extent of 'extortion' and all that would be 'charged' which would be shameful on humanity. When any professional conduct would suffer from such a 'state of mind' and gets dominating over and above 'everything' then any kind of rules or regulations would not be in a position to contain such tendency. There is no injustice at all till we are charging a 'reasonable price' in our profession in accordance with our professional 'capacity' and 'expertise'. It becomes a gross injustice when in blind race of professionalism keeping aside our professional expertise and standards we 'did' and 'charged' all that which had nothing to do with our professional capacity. Leave it, alright still up to this stage but when with a dishonest intention under the 'color' of our professional 'conduct' and expertise we do all that by breaching trust of people which our professional ethics never permits. Under such circumstances definitely it is a culpable crime and law of the land will take its course of action.

To follow the professional conduct is a tough and strict spiritual process. To control the 'greed' of charging price is not that easy. Now such cases of serious violations of professional ethics are coming into light as a very common phenomenon. Where the patient is to be 'operated upon' for any stomach ailment. Patient is lying at the operation table before the doctor. He is made unconscious. During the process of operation and without the knowledge of the patient his one of the kidney is stolen away dishonestly and his stomach stitched afterwards. So simple as that for such professionals. Now it is left up to you as to by which 'spec' of humanity this criminal 'trafficking' in human organs should be seen? There are reports of 'expert' professionals facilitating criminal gangs dealing in trafficking of human organs. Innocent children would be kidnapped from society. Under 'supervision' of professional experts important organs from the body of children would be taken out and their dead bodies would be 'buried' or thrown away somewhere in 'nallahs' only to be eaten away by vultures. If law happens to be 'active' and they are taken into custody the moment there would be a long row of 'expert legal advice' from law professionals. Legal experts will also be paid 'full price' of their professional advice in assisting the other professionals. The culprits have to be saved from the clutches of law. Come what may? What is to be done? In criminal matters creating a situation of doubt is not that tough job for law experts. This in fact is their profession. They very well know this fact that the law 'in fact' is blind. Once a doubtful situation has been created into the 'matter' the law is bound to exonerate the culprit by giving him the benefit of doubt. Who does not want to be exonerated? Ethics 'going professional' would be fully 'paid' for it after all. May be it is being done at the cost of justice. But how does it make any difference? No way.

"Ethics getting professional means now the limits of humanity would also be thrashed out. The price of 'labor' would be fully charged with to an extent of 'extortion' and all that would be 'charged' which would be shameful on humanity. When any professional conduct would suffer from such a 'state of mind' and gets dominating over and above 'everything' then any kind of rules or regulations would not be in a position to contain such tendency."

94

Sectors of Primary Health

Can we correlate sectors of primary health with the fundamental right of a person to life? Under Article 21 of the Constitution of India the fundamental right to life includes the right to live with decency and right to live a healthy life. Soundness of health of its citizen should be the primary consideration under any welfare state. Sound health is *sine qua non* of sound life with human dignity and confers strength in true sense to the fundamental right to life. This is keeping in conformity with the spirit behind it. Role of health sectors are very significant for a better and decent human living. A life without health is no life. High level researches in the fields of medical sciences have no doubt increased longevity among people but with heavy dependency on medicines. For strength of the nation we need to ensure to have 'health with life' and not that to have 'life without health'.

The state of affairs of primary health sectors in our rural and semi-urban areas is very pathetic. In urban areas and other big cities health related facilities may be satisfactorily adequate but looking to the rural masses requirements, the facilities of primary health centers are much less than adequate. Merely opening up of primary health centers in villages would not serve the purpose unless medical infrastructural facilities are also ensured at continuous pace. It has been noticed that at majority of primary health centers even basic first aid medical facilities are not available, what to talk about infrastructural medical facilities? Moreover, the government doctors who are posted at these primary health centers by means of 'government orders' remain absent. Although they report their joining at the place of posting and keep getting their salary regularly but do not come for 'duties' even for 'weeks' and 'months' altogether.

They are seen moving around centre only during the day of payment of their salary. Where the governments make an arrangement 'facilitating' transfer of their salaries directly in their bank accounts then they become more free from their obligations even to visit their primary health centers occasionally. It is also noticed that if four or five doctors are posted at any primary health centre located in rural areas they would make such a mutual 'understanding' among themselves that out of the five governments doctors only one would come at the centre on a single day and the rest of the four would follow alternatively. This way their individual next visit to the centre only after sixth day. All the five doctors and other paramedical staff are very rarely present during so-called inspection visits of higher ups at the centre. We can easily imagine pathetic conditions on those primary health centers where hardly two or three government doctors are posted. Where they fail to reach upon any such mutual arrangement then the primary health centre remains 'closed' without any doctor. Looking to the gross negligence of doctors towards their duty the paramedical staff at the centre also goes careless openly. Because the doctors have already lost their moral authority to check and discipline the paramedical staff for the reasons that they themselves are careless. Stories of primary health centers in India goes like this only.

Let us not talk about non-availability of infrastructural facilities at these centers for reasons of either no regular supply of power or interrupted supply of power for major part of the day. Rural ambulance services are very poor and are seen running without much infrastructure. It is found that government ambulance services more act like 'touts' of private nursing home in cities. Government ambulance service handlers are 'paid handsomely' by private nursing homes for supplying them patients. At times where ambulance services are needed most in emergency for any serious patient either they do not reach for petty excuses or even when they reach by that time the inmates of the patient make some other alternative arrangement to rush the patient to hospital in the city. Sometimes many serious patients pass away on the spot waiting for ambulance to come or they die while on their way to the hospital for the reasons of delay in getting ambulance services. The sectors of primary health have to play a major role in protecting and ensuring healthy life to the infants and other growing children in rural areas. Numbers of children suffer from malnutrition right from their infancy due to the reasons of poverty. They will grow weak through their young age. Keeping in mind the data that seventy percent of the population lives in villages then what will happen to entire nation's health should be a matter of serious concern for us? Proper health means healthy body and healthy mind. Otherwise we should keep ready to be a weak nation. We need 'comprehensive' health to the people at large.

> *"The sectors of primary health have to play a major role in protecting and ensuring healthy life to the infants and other growing children in rural areas. Numbers of children suffer from malnutrition right from their infancy due to the reasons of poverty. They will grow weak through their young age."*

95

Starvation Death Situations

If in today's modern era of science and technology situations become like that people are 'dying' due to starvation. Then just imagine why people will not develop the feeling to revolt against the system? Who is bothered if people are starving to death? Hunger relates to existence of human life. By not taking food for a single day some may happen to experience the pain of hunger. It is ridiculous as if they are making 'mockery' of it by claiming this way that they too experience pain of hunger. Then few statements would be made full with 'compassion' expressing their concern that this hunger needs to be eradicated from this earth. First hunger of every individual is mitigated then only one could say that hunger would be eradicated from this earth. Death due to starvation does not mean that when dead body of the person is taken away then only we would be able to understand that the particular individual died of starvation eventually. Hunger and starvation are two different situations. There is no such instance of any starvation death in medical sciences that a person did not have bread to eat today and he died by the evening or tomorrow due to hunger. And it happened so all of sudden that our 'public welfare system' could not take notice of it. Otherwise system would have definitely 'managed' to provide him 'bread' for the day and would not allow him to starve to death. Why it would have let him die of hunger? Ssh..! Had people's death due to hunger been so all of sudden? The system gets so alert that it does not let any individual die of hunger. Who would be bothered if people are starving to death? Can't help. Unfortunate people. Live only to starve and die.

Process of starving to death is a continuous human process. It is not the result of living in hunger for a day or two. Individuals used to die of hunger daily bit a bit. Then after months and years of this state, lastly one day his dead body is taken away for 'disposal'. Then only it comes to the notice of the system that he would have died of hunger. But for 'administrative reasons' system is still not ready to accept that to be a death due to hunger. The system managers take number of days in keep denying this very fact. They do not find themselves in a position to believe it. How can it happen after all? How can he die of hunger? They keep them addressing that they issued lot many such 'government orders' that no person be let die of hunger. He must have died of some disease but not of hunger. Rest assures. Why the system need to accept this fact that if the person suffered the pain of hunger for months then his body must be diseased only after all? The system is not ready to accept it that the 'disease' could be 'hunger borne' itself. If it did happen then the system would be in docks. Before it becomes 'clear' that person's disease was borne due to continuous hunger only, system 'hurriedly manages' his last rites for his 'heavenly' abode. Why do we not understand system's public 'welfare' angle in performing last rites of the person with a heavenly feel? This is disgusting. We should stop our habits in putting the system in 'docks' time and again for petty reasons. The system too, after all, has its own limitations? Why do not we try to understand its limits? We should not find faults with others. We should discover our own 'destiny' if it is poor and make out efforts to get rid of it.

If we or our kids are to live in 'hunger' then why the system is to be blamed for it? If due to poverty we are not able to manage our bread then how the system can help it out? Our destiny is to be blamed all that. We failed to born with 'silver spoon' in our mouth. Now there is no way to come out of it. However, one should be always proud of his birth even if born in a poor family. That's the mark of self-respect may be very rare. For decades system is worried about that poverty should be removed. One after the other they are busy keep launching poverty eradication schemes. People should get bread and there is no occasion for starvation deaths. Not necessary where the person is hungry of 'five' breads he should feel satisfied that system gets him 'two' breads at least'

Rest of his 'empty' stomach he should fill with water. At least he will not die. Yes..! May be he gets weaker. No problem. But do not let him to die.

What to do? How much they should manage? To whom and how many numbers they should keep worrying for? Population has even gone increasing in billions. The ball is in the court of the people now, what the system can do? Planning commission with its full integrity 'launched' many poverty eradication programs. Lot of time and energy was 'wasted' by them in keep moving the 'poverty line' up and down. But still there was no scope visible to get rid of poverty. Even by keep bringing poverty line 'down and down' still if 'thirty percent' population are cursed to remain 'below poverty line' only then planning commissions should not be held responsible for it. Their job is to keep planning and they are doing their job 'sincerely' planning and planning. To remove hunger and poverty eradication if programs like rural employment guarantee, mid-day meals, subsidy in food grains are 'gifted' to system borne corruption then all those who indulge in such corruption are also an integral part of this system only. They too have their own shares in such programs. How long they would keep on implementing these programs 'empty' handed? What they are going to 'get' if people's poverty is removed? System has no control over them. In fact we did commit mistake in understanding that perhaps system would screw them? But our understanding proved to be wrong. We forgot that they all are 'system' in themselves. Who will dare to control them? What control..? First they would 'strengthen' them by filling their stomach up to the neck. Then afterwards if something is 'left behind' they would be able to think of helping some hungry poor. If hungry poor happen to die then what the kind of help they would do to them? Why do we forget that charity first begins at home only? System caretakers need to be told that poor fellow citizen do not live on mercy of their 'charity' but constitutionally they have fundamental right to live. Its system's constitutional liability to remove situations of starvation from Indian society.

"Process of starving to death is a continuous human process. It is not the result of living in hunger for a day or two. Individuals used to die of hunger daily bit a bit. Then after months and years of this state, lastly one day his dead body is taken away

for 'disposal'. Then only it comes to the notice of the system that he would have died of hunger. But for 'administrative reasons' system is still not ready to accept that to be a death due to hunger. The system managers take number of days in keep denying this very fact. They do not find themselves in a position to believe it. How can it happen after all? How can he die of hunger?"

———————————————

96

To Live With Human Dignity

How does it sound if we talk about fundamental right of people to live with human dignity? No doubt at least it sounds good. Under laws matters relating to fundamental rights are taken very seriously. The basic or fundamental rights under Constitutional Law of nations are considered to be among prime rights conferred to citizens. If persons not being citizen of that nation still the fundamental law provides certain rights to non-citizen as well which are linked with human existence? Fundamental rights could be defined as those rights which are guaranteed by fundamental law of the land and are very essential for human life. Without these rights a person in his life cannot think of living with human dignity. Significance of fundamental rights could be understood in the sense that under legal system special provision are prescribed for enforcement of these rights. In matters of violation of these rights the higher courts have been conferred with constitutional remedial jurisdiction of direct hearing through 'special writs' bypassing the lower courts. A person in society could lead his life with human dignity this itself is an important fundamental right.

What do we mean by human dignity? It is simple thing that at very first sight a clear distinction should be 'visible' in the life of a human being as distinct from an animal like life. If you are not able to distinguish in any society about the life of a 'human' and a human living in 'animal like' conditions then it is left up to you as to what kind of 'human dignity' you would be able to search in such life living conditions? In the vicinity of modern societies people are cursed to live in jhuggi-jhoparis. At least once you need to go there just to see that in what kind of 'definition' of human dignity they should be put like? The people living in these jhuggi-jhoparis and their daily pitiable conditions are totally 'not visible' to our governments while moving across. This cannot even be claimed. There could be blindness in 'government arrogance' but they do not become 'that blind' which renders them difficult to run their governments. After all they have to run their governments? They have to talk 'something' about humanity and then 'keep making' efforts to put them through implementation. It would not be necessary that their efforts are going to be successful only. But efforts are being made continuously it should be visible to people anyhow. We innocent people often are not able to distinguish and understand whether keep on looking the efforts being done is more important or else some changes must be looking visible also as result of those efforts at the ground level realities? If a blunt lie has been 'orchestrated' as truth hundred many times then it starts appearing to be like truth. To whom should we blame? Our modern system management has moved on this track only. Whether efforts are being made or not? Or whatever it is? Making such efforts appearing to be is so 'advertised' and 'propagandized' that we go confused doubtlessly. You can refer it to be a cleverly 'psychological dose' of the system. The system's beating around eradicating poverty for 'decades' had been the kind of propaganda that we truly started 'expecting' that their such efforts which appear to be would perhaps change the ground realities. The human who were forced to live life even worse than animals probably would get some human dignity. Would start getting a 'piece' of bread peacefully? But it all proved to be the same 'blunt lie' which if repeated hundred many times starts creating an impression as if it is true. Thrashed and scattered around in a 'single stroke' not left like to be restored even.

On road sides in every city could be easily seen 'filthy garbage' from around the city is dumped. It makes the atmosphere all 'stinking' unbearable to breathe while moving around due to viral decomposition. Should I humbly put before you the ground realities of human dignity? Feel obliged for the permission granted. Honestly speaking you might have also witnessed while moving across these dumped stinking garbage. In the same stinking dump garbage are seen the children of human beings along with crows, vultures, street dogs and pigs? The children 'searching' for their futures in the dumps hours altogether. After witnessing such scenes we should not talk about human dignity and also about the fundamental rights of persons to live with human dignity. Our human kids are clearly seen 'struggling' life worst than animals even. Where they will live and where they will die. The governments might have also 'seen' them in stinking garbs through their 'coated windows' of vehicles while moving across. We are told that our system managers are properly trained to take care of such things that our governments should not be moved across such roadsides where dumpy stinking humanity is seen visible worst than animals. It may 'infect' the highly sensitive governments. If the governments are to move after all across such roadsides unavoidably then also system managers are perfectly trained to get the stinking garbage 'removed' overnight and dumped 'elsewhere' at least for that one day. With red carpets and perfumes sprayed all around. The governments are made to pass through red carpets in an atmosphere filled with perfumes. Red carpets are then to be 'uncovered' immediately after the government fleets have passed through. The next day only dumping of garbage starts piling up only to further stink and stink. The 'humanity' again gets busy with it around animals and the 'human dignity' itself is 'dumped' within the stinking garbage. Why should we not admit this bare truth honestly that in fact we are living in a fool's paradise? We should talk about their fundamental rights only later. If system could get them with some human dignity only then they should think of some justice for them in the name of humanity sake. Let us hope for the best always.

"If you are not able to distinguish in any society about the life of a 'human' and a human living in 'animal like' conditions then it is left up to you as to what kind of 'human dignity' you would be able to search in such life living conditions? In the vicinity of modern societies people are cursed to live in jhuggi-jhoparis. At least once you need to go there just to see that in what kind of 'definition' of human dignity they should be put like?"

97

Look for the Incapables!

Who will look for the people who are incapable? It is very difficult to define incapacity. Any person could have physical incapacity or mental incapacity. Few have physical or mental incapacity since birth. Born incapacities are not within control of the person and he is destined to carry such incapacities through his life. Do we consider it as nature borne injustice? It is very difficult to say that. We should draw our attention to such incapacities also which are not purely nature born and are 'system born'. Probably the person would not have become victim of such incapacity had the system not been careless? For instance persons became victims of criminal activities taking place in the society. Even after medical treatment he suffered from physical incapacity. In the opinion of the doctors his incapacity was now permanent in nature and would continue for life. There are several similar examples where people go 'handicapped' by getting victims of accidents which take place due to carelessness of the system. In such train or bus accidents the people who become handicapped the concerned government departments feel get relieved from their 'accountability' after payment of 'compensation' to them. Such cases also come into light where payment of compensation remains merely a pure political announcement. After lot many trouble and running around system managers the person gets some portion of compensation while rest of it is distributed among corrupt system caretakers.

Under the law the question is always of accountability. If it is system's accountability to stop crimes in society then whether the state was successful in stopping crimes? If not then why should people happen to suffer for failures of the system? And became victims of the crime some way or the other and go incapables? The incapacity may be in the form of total disability or partial disability of the person. It will depend upon seriousness of physical injury caused to the person by the crime. Else the poor standard of medical treatment rendered to him and negligence thereafter would also determine the level of incapacity. Medical negligence contributes in enhancing degree of disability. Looking to our prevailing socio-economic situations in such accidental cases or to the victims of criminal activities, there is no guarantee that high level medical treatment would be available to them. In government hospitals too there are no less examples of medical negligence. Our system has still not become so high standard that it would provide better treatment to such persons in private hospitals on its own expenses. Under such circumstances people allow themselves to be at the hands of the system only and leaving rest to their destiny. Majority of population in our society are not economically that capable to bear it all on their own. Again the same question arises as to who will bother for the people who are incapable?

Whether it is born disability, system born or due to any other reason the truth is that the person gets incapacitated. Whether he is able to live his life in a dignified manner or not? Talking about it all probably would amount to ridicule his helplessness. If person's incapacity comes in the category of 'total disability' now he will not be able to earn the livelihood of his family members in a proper manner. Whilst his 'partial disability' would also keep on adversely affecting his capacity to earn. Where in society a person has been murdered by criminals. A number of people are killed in 'collective violence' following bomb blasts in terror attacks people go handicapped badly due to serious physical injuries. People die while they became victims of accidents, crimes. Under such situations their entire family goes incapacitated. Since the person who has been murdered or killed was the only bread earning member in that family. Now what you will say about the 'collective total disability' of such families? Yes..! This is a bitter truth. Do we expect from children and women members of such families that now they should come out from their homes to work? What to expect? Who is now there to feed their children? The tragedy is that they are forced to come out otherwise they will starve to death.

There are people in the categories of socio-economically weaker sections of the society. Should we not admit that socio-economic weakness does make them disable? They continue to be in weaker sections of the society for years and years altogether. Does it not make them disable? The people not getting benefits of 'welfare schemes' of a 'welfare state' on the ground root levels. Does it not make them disable? Their kids remaining undernourished, uneducated and weak. Whether it would make them capable of anymore? Whether they would remain cursed to 'live as incapables' throughout and 'die as incapables' only? Disability is not by the reasons of physical or mental handicaps only. So the system does not get to excuse of itself and feel absolved of all its liabilities. Bad system generates social disabilities. Such disabilities are irreparable in nature unless system gets out of its sleep. The incapacity of socio-economically weaker classes completely comes within the ambit of socio-economic handicap. The way physical and mental handicap weakens a person exactly in the same manner collective socio-economic handicaps weakens the entire social system and ultimately weakens the nation. Who will look after and take care of the people who are born incapables, became incapables during their life due to accident or crimes or else socially incapables for the reasons of socio-economic weakness? Who is there..! Who could do justice to them? Who is listening to it? Is there anybody? Social justice to remove thrust incapacities and forced social disabilities.

"Whether it is born disability, system born or due to any other reason the truth is that the person gets incapacitated. Whether he is able to live his life in a dignified manner or not? Talking about it all probably would amount to ridicule his helplessness. If person's incapacity comes in the category of 'total disability' now he will not be able to earn the livelihood of his family members in a proper manner. Whilst his 'partial disability' would also keep on adversely affecting his capacity to earn."

98

Distributive Justice

D istributive Justice is the term which represents 'just distribution' of goods among the members of society and also it refers to fairness of one's outcomes. Distribution relates to be 'need based' and that is only judicious. Where distribution of goods is more than needed or is less than needed creates situations of injustice. Keeping the constitutional parameters in mind what the system has been made is that such a systematic society should be established where welfare of people are ensured and it should be effectively protected. Social systems should be like that in which justice social, economical and political should reflect in all the institutions of national life. State needs to see in particular that 'disparity in income' of the people should be eliminated and inequalities in social status, facilities and of opportunities should be removed. Such arrangements also need be made for such groups of people who reside in different areas or engaged in different vocations. May be due to factors of nature the life levels of people living in different areas could not have become equal to the levels of people residing in other developed or developing areas. There could be local or geographical backwardness. To eliminate it all the state would have to make sincere efforts. May be the people engaged in different vocations are not earning income proportionate to their labor put in. People do have full capacity to work hard but due to inadequate vocational training or its being of low standard productive capacity of these people is reduced considerably. Their capacity to work hard could not be properly utilized. Inequality continues to prevail. It is for responsible state agencies to exploit for the potential of our youth by putting in them proper training.

With a view to ensure justice the 'state' need to go far fair distribution of state's resources in those areas and make available fair vocational training to those group of people who despite having the capacity to work hard are unable to increase their productive potential. They do not get full return of their labor. Then 'frustration' makes its grip without much delay. Probably the system is not that sensitive that it takes cognizance of their frustration well before sufficient time is left. They start 'deviating' by the time it gets too late. Perhaps the system too does not have any such prompt planning that at least it could distribute 'fair training' itself to these hard workers which could have enabled them for self employment. They are willing to do hard work. Whether the system itself is at fault in it? If the system has with itself some concrete distributive system plans then system should come forward? If inequalities in social status continue or it exhibits increasing patterns. If disparity in incomes continues or registers growth in it then it endorses this very fact that there appears to be scarcity of any such concrete plan? If claim of system is that there were plans not only from today but for last so many years, then their impact should be visible? Where is the impact of distribution at least if not an equal one? Its justifiable distribution should be ensured? It would be concluded then if supposing system has plans but still meaningful results are not coming out of it then under such circumstances now it is found duly endorsed that honest enforcement of these plans is certainly proved to be defective.

Distributive justice should see that every citizen women and men, rich and poor have equal and adequate means of livelihood. Control of community material resources and their best distribution should be done for 'common good' of people. The economic system of country should not be conducted in a manner so that as a result of it wealth of country and other areas of production remain concentrated only within chosen 'few hands' and the 'common man' fails to get nothing in his favor even in the name of distribution. The spirit of distributive justice remains limited merely on papers. It is very dangerous situation for 'distributive interests' of common man. 'Equal pay for equal work' should not be seen in terms of 'discrimination' with reference to women and men. Changes as a result of plans appear but even today this discrimination is clearly visible among working classes where labor is not organized. The welfare state has enacted labor laws but so what? Unorganized labor has to face worst kind of discrimination and exploitation at the hands of so-called equalitarian society. Women workers are victims of gender discrimination and distribution of justice does not reach them. Distributive justice should express its concern that our worker's health particularly health of women workers and child labor should not be jeopardized. Exploitation of their physical labor should not be done in a manner that for their economic necessities they be forced to do any such work which does not suit to their age or physical health. But it is noticed that it does not happen? Welfare of our women and child labor are not protected. Work is reported to be taken from children in hazardous occupations. Please do not say it is due to economic compulsion of such children. It is shameful that our children are putting in hard labor in their delicate age and we are simply sitting silent. When there will be honest planning in favor of such children and other neglected ones who is there to stop implementation? When would come policies for equal distribution of education and mental development to these children? It remains to be seen. If it is claimed that plans are there very much then till date why are we not getting expected results? It would be better that let the system itself make it clear?

The system can never deny from this fact or even claim that social inequalities or economic disparities are completely under control. Eliminating such inequalities in a distributive justice system will be seen with time. But delays in 'eliminations' are not tolerable. Why do we lose our hope? That's true but where is the ray of hope? In the name of voice of its inner conscience the system should at least make an honest analysis of this very fact as to why all is not well? At least on the basis of data prepared by the Planning Commission system should make it clear whether socio-economic inequalities are being 'seen' to be eliminated? Please do not tell for the sake of records. System should show in actual physical terms. Not in terms of paper data. Please come forward with an authentic reply. Remember..! If distribution is not done 'judiciously' in proportion to needs of 'we the people' then there are indications of 'civil war' like situations. We need to avoid any such civil war. Take necessary 'corrective steps' before it is too late.

"In the name of voice of its inner conscience the system should at least make an honest analysis of this very fact as to why all is not well? At least on the basis of data prepared by the Planning Commission system should make it clear whether socio-economic inequalities are being 'seen' to be eliminated? Please do not tell for the sake of records. System should show in actual physical terms. Not in terms of paper data. Please come forward with an authentic reply. Remember..! If distribution is not done 'judiciously' in proportion to needs of 'we the people' then there are indications of 'civil war' like situations. We need to avoid any such civil war. Take necessary 'corrective steps' before it is too late."

99

Fundamental Right to Good Governance

Good governance is much talked about agenda now-a-days. It sounds good too. It would be very rare that people are not influenced by initiatives taken for good governance. If today we openly talk for the necessities of good governance then we apparently admit this very fact that we are lacking in good governance. No good governance means bad governance. In a democratic system like us if there is a government to govern then off course need not to say it must be good governance only. We the people have a fundamental right to good governance. The constitutional parameters make it expressly clear that fundamental rights or other legal rights are made enforceable by law so is the fundamental right to good governance. People must get their fundamental right to good governance. If they are being denied from it they should demand it and get it enforced through legal system of the country.

In present global as well as national perspectives 'governance' and 'good governance' has been attributed to international development literature. Good governance has direct bearing upon development of human civilizations. Our society has been witness to it that root cause of all the evils relating to societal development has been 'bad governance'. Governance means the process of 'decision making' and the process by which decisions are put into force. Good governance reflects in global development and becomes basis for international classifications such as developed countries, developing countries, lesser or least developed countries. Whether it is seen at national or international levels human development in a judicious manner is only possible when the system 'honestly' and 'sincerely' ensures 'good governance' in the society. It concerns with development of greater quality of life for human beings.

There may be varied dimensions of human development. But specifically from angles of good governance the 'concept of human development' disperses the concentration of distribution of 'goods' and 'services' that 'under privileged' people need. The basic capabilities for human development are to lead long and healthy lives. To be knowledgeable and educated. To have access to resources and social services needed for decent standards of human living and to be able to participate in the life of the community. Good governance could be best understood when we compare 'ineffective economies' and 'ineffective political bodies' with 'flourishing economics' and 'healthy political bodies'. Ineffective economies and careless political bodies attribute to their failures when during decision making and its implementation they start discriminating between 'select groups' of society and the 'deprived masses' at large. Where there are apparent 'social exclusions' the need of justice is that good governance should always have a deep concern for 'social inclusions'. An accountability has been thrust upon the governments for good governance through judicious involvement of all the 'stakeholders' not only in 'decision making' but in its 'effective implementation' too.

The good governance should not be misunderstood for the concept of right to be given or to be taken thereafter. Good governance is a specific kind of 'delivery of justice' at its highest levels. It should be made categorically clear that unless the characteristics like participation, consensus orientation, accountability, transparency, responsiveness, effective and efficient, equitable and inclusiveness and the rule of law are followed the objectives of good governance are bound to be defeated and the most sufferer class would be the common man. Who has nothing to lose but hopelessly looks for some rightful gains towards his meaningful survival on this earth.

Its people's right to have a corruption free society. The good governance should assure that corruption is minimized in public life if not eradicated completely. The views of minorities are also taken into account while performing the task of decision making and its final implementation at the grass root levels. The most worrying question is whether who will represent the voices of the most vulnerable ones in the society? It should be taken as warning signal that voices of the 'most vulnerable' ones should be heard in the decision making and its implementation. Otherwise with the passage of time facing all 'exclusions' in governance a major group would develop in society and pose a big challenge to the caretakers of good governance. It may sound strange but bitterly true. There are reports of 'crime syndicates' influencing decision making and destroying the ends of good governance. This needs to be stopped particularly when criminals successfully make their entry into political bodies. We urgently require a 'sustainable human development' which is possible only through judicious good governance which is able to ensure its advantages even to the last man on this earth. So...! Help us God..!!!

"Its people's right to have a corruption free society. The good governance should assure that corruption is minimized in public life if not eradicated completely. The views of minorities are also taken into account while performing the task of decision making and its final implementation at the grass root levels. The most worrying question is whether who will represent the voices of the most vulnerable ones in the society?"